Naked
L i b e r t y

Memoirs of My Childhood

Guided by Passion
Educated by Wild Horses

The Language of Movement, Communication, and
Leadership Through the Way of Horses

by
Carolyn Resnick

Published by
Amigo Publications, Inc.
PO Box 666
Los Olivos, CA 93441-0666

ISBN: 0-9658533-4-9

Library of Congress Control Number: 2004116377

Resnick, Carolyn, 2005

Naked Liberty
by Carolyn Resnick

First Edition 2005

Cover photo by Karen Anderson

Printed in U.S.A.

Table of Contents

Book Three
Educated by Wild Horses

Book Four
The Language of Movement, Communication, and Leadership Through the Ways of Horses

Dedication

I dedicate this book to my mother, Paulina Francetic.

I remember a lesson my mother shared with me on the beauty of nature from seeing a single rose. When I had just begun to walk on my own, my mother took me out to her rose garden when the rose buds were beginning to mature. She picked a rose bud, handed it to me and said, "Is it not fantastic, roses in the desert!" She took the budding flower and pulled off the green sepals, exposing the bright red unborn rosebud perched on top of the green stem like a teardrop. She announced that this was what the word "beautiful" meant. I admired it all morning. It was truly a red, red rose with an important message. I learned how to appreciate the beauty in nature from the expression of my mother's joy and her sharing this experience with me.

Without her guidance through my childhood, I could not have found the universal connection of all things nor could I have found the secret society of wild horses, nor been accepted into their family with pecking order rights, nor learned the language of horses, nor could I have written this book.

My mother influenced me to be a student of nature searching for the harmony and beauty that exist in every moment. From her strength in the middle of chaos she knows where to put her energy and focus while staying connected to source and personal power. Paulina, my mother, knows when it is time to love and when it is time to endure. My family refers to her as Mother Nature because to us she seems as powerful and as supportive. I never once witnessed my mother ever stepping out of the Garden of Eden or longing for anything more.

Carolyn Resnick

Acknowledgments

In no time at all I discovered that a ghostwriter was not going to be able to write my book. What I wanted to say had to come from me. I went for help to my long-time friend, Penelope Sky, who has a masters degree in English Literature. She told me to write my feelings down and not to worry about the rules of grammar and punctuation. I spent a few days at her home and she gave me lessons in writing. She had me sit down at her kitchen table and write a few sentences on a small piece of paper like a note you would pass in a classroom. She asked me to hand it to her folded. She took the note and read it. She then interpreted in her own words what she thought my notes said and asked me if that was what I meant. She then went on telling me how the note made her feel and she asked me if that was how I wanted her to feel. Many times it wasn't, but little by little, I got clearer in my writing. I had some learning disabilities as the school system had failed to teach me what I needed to learn. Penelope's guidance gave me the ability to write this book.

My down-the-street neighbor Kevin, a skilled writer whom I admired as a true artist, coached me patiently with each chapter, telling me how wonderful a writer I was, no matter how good or bad the chapters were. She inspired me to get in touch with the writer I am today. She also put the book on a computer and listened to me read each chapter so we could work together in a creative process. Those days were special and are the reason I was able to express my inner experiences to the reader. Kevin was the greatest contributor to the writing of *Naked Liberty*.

I moved from Sonoma to Southern California; there, I met Mona

Patton, a true horse lover who was looking for a method to train horses that expressed the love and companionship she experienced with her horse every day. We worked together with her eight Quarter Horses developing her horsemanship skills, and she helped me edit my book because she felt it was an important contribution to the horse community.

Penelope Sky, Kevin, and Mona Patton are the team that helped me through the process. I am forever grateful for the experience we all shared together.

I read the book to most of my friends to get their impressions. I valued their opinions and their input helped the direction of my focus and stories.

All of you will remember your contributions to the development of the chapters. Thank you for your help.

Karen Sheets, a friend and student of mine who in her own right is an animal and horse communicator, helped the most with my story development. Her bird, Buddy, and DJ, her best friend, an Arabian mare, played a part in my everyday life at the time I was writing my book. Thank you for the companionship between the pages.

I am forever grateful for the help and support of Laurie and Michael Parker. To Laurie, a special thanks for being there for me beyond the call of duty, supporting my work with her excellent understanding of the written word. And to Michael for keeping the campfires burning during the process.

To Neda De Mayo, Christine Cole, Carey Schulman, Libby Oullett, Kendal Comfort, India and her father Robert Gomez, Baquieta Parker, Horse Dancer Vincent Spiaggia, Ted Adel, Sonia Struggia. In gratitude, some of the wild horses' names were changed to the names of the horses of some of the people who supported the direction of the book. Thanks gang!!

A special thanks to Robin Gates, a friend and a student of mine who spanned the entire process of the writing of the book, who honored my work by becoming an outstanding horsewoman of my methods and guided me to be in peace with the process of my life.

In the final touches of *Naked Liberty*, I would like to thank Heinz Reusser, publisher and editor of *Conquistador, the World of the Spanish Horses*, for the encouragement and inspiration he freely gave.

Thanks to Paul Robinson for his large contribution to the edit. To Kathleen Martin, Ph D, of the team of Professional Services for the

Acknowledgements

Ken Blanchard Companies, for her help in developing the Leader of Leaders chapter. To Laurin Augdon for her moral support and for helping in the promotion of the book. To Jeanette Correia for the last read. To Jill Keating who led me to the magical map.

Thanks to Behrooz Danadoost, my spiritual adviser, who kept me on my path of pure potentiality and plugged into the universal connection of all things and reminded me that my job in life is to follow my passion and continue.

And lastly, a huge thanks to *California Riding Magazine* for their support, Erin Gilmore for her final edit, and Michael Brown for his book design.

Carolyn Resnick

Prologue

One morning, while out walking, I met a large bobcat. We surprised each other at the end of a tree-lined path. We were fifteen feet apart. I was delighted to have run across him. Bobcats are elusive by nature. What amazed me was that he didn't run. Instead, he appeared alarmed for only a second and then he accepted my presence by joining me on my walk.

He was in a playful mood as we walked together and expressed it with a jaunty stride as he smelled plants, tussled around in the dust, and leaped about, catching invisible prey. He walked ahead, then waited for me to catch up to him. When I got ahead, I waited for him. Eventually he lost interest and ambled into the distance, crossing a dry riverbed.

I often wondered what his version of our story would be. I asked this question to wild horses and they told me their story. Their story set me on a journey that has lasted a lifetime. A journey few people have traveled. I was looking for the harmony that I could share with horses in their world. I wanted to learn about the community needs of horses and how nature and the elements support their well-being and develop their behavior. I was also looking for a universal harmonious connection to the world of animals through a language and values we might have in common.

I wasn't looking for the dog-eat-dog side of nature like in the book *Moby Dick* by Herman Melville. Man's struggle with nature and the elements could be greatly reduced if we understood that harmony is the natural condition in nature. If we saw that nature is there to support our needs, we would not challenge nature as much. The natural condition in nature and in relationships in nature is harmony. Chaos will eventually return itself to harmony. Just as tossing a pebble in a quiet pond stirs up ripples, in time, the pond's surface returns to its normal harmonious state.

Carl Sagan said, "In the future, man will have to communicate with animals to survive." The difference between humans and animals is their perception of nature. For humans, nature is a challenge. For animals, nature is home. The title of my book, *Naked Liberty,* is a statement of this difference between humans and animals in their relationship to nature. Living in the natural elements, we feel naked and even trapped while animals in nature feel free and at liberty. If we understood companionship as well as we understood competition, we would see that nature is a team player not to be conquered, but is instead an essential part of abundance.

I call my method of horse training Liberty Training, Byond the Whisper™. Another reason I titled my book *Naked Liberty* is because "naked liberty" means to me that when my horse and I are connected in movements in companionship interactions, the horse and I, in my mind, are in a state of "naked liberty." In those moments I am in true harmony with my horse and the performance we are sharing together.

The stories I will be sharing with you are memoirs from my childhood of communicating with wild and domestic horses. My adventures were filled with discovery and lessons I learned that developed my ability to communicate with horses.

Some readers will purely enjoy my adventures with horses as a child and revel in my experiences in nature, while others will want to find the deeper meaning and purpose behind my stories. For those looking for the lessons hidden in my stories, I have outlined their purpose in the following pages. If you are not interested in the underlying lessons, you may want to proceed to the introduction.

The first half of the book consists of stories that give the reader the opportunity to look at horses and nature through my eyes so we may travel the journey together into a wild horse herd. From the stories you will gain practical knowledge of horse behavior and problem solving. The second half of the book focuses on my experiences with wild horses, starting at the bottom of the pecking order and working my way up. From my relationship with the wild horses, I learned I could ride a wild horse from a bonded trust.

The book focuses on three subjects. First, it guides horse people in their ability to express their love in an appropriate way which fosters their horse's respect, friendship, and desire to accept their leadership. Second, it guides equestrians in how to use horse training formulas more effectively. Third, it guides readers in leadership and communication skills with humans.

The stories are intended to create a shift in the reader's perception by focusing on the love of nature and wild horse behavior, which in turn creates a greater understanding of pecking order rituals horses use. I believe understanding pecking order rituals is the key to getting along with horses.

Through my childhood experiences with horses, I discovered a code of behavior that horses and humans have in common. Seeing the similarity of horse and human behavior demystifies training and communicating with horses. After reading this book you will have information on how to create willing relationships with horses and humans that stem from a universal need everyone has to follow a leader. Understanding the social behavior of horses enables one to better communicate leadership that is fair, just, moral and effective.

How I learned to identify what was fair, just, moral and effective was by following rules of leadership that I felt were ethical behavior on my part. The rules I followed were the rules the horses set for me when I was a child and horses could tell me what to do. I had to be likable and gain favor as a leader with the horse I was working with, which caused me to communicate with him only when he wanted me to. I learned how to create horses' interest in wanting to follow my lead through the bond I developed with them. This ability to create harmony led me to the art of leadership and the willingness of a horse to perform and follow my lead.

Leadership has nothing to do with force. The stories in this book show how I gained control and respect of specific horses I encountered as a child. Even though they had a clear advantage over me in size and strength, I was able to gain their respect and cooperation.

The book shows the importance of many hours of observations and my failures getting the wild horses to first accept my presence. The process that I went through will shed light on why horses are often hard to train. I needed to get the horses to accept me as a family member and I had to discover from my observations how to achieve this acceptance. Once the horses accepted me, working with them was much easier. Before wild horses would respond to me like they did with each other, I had to develop a bond with them and take my position at the bottom of the pecking order. From there I learned proper behavior of lead horses.

Naked Liberty goes into the social behavior of wild horses and into details of how the pecking order rituals and reprimand work together creating a leadership where reprimand is never necessary.

The reason I told my story in *Naked Liberty* rather than a how-to book is that I believe my experiences are more revealing in how to relate to horses than a how-to book would be. I believe that experience is our greatest teacher and the guided experience is extremely valuable.

I was lucky growing up with a family who had horse sense and raised me to find my own way by allowing me to learn on my own as they monitored my experiences. What my family knew was that the most important thing was to shape my character and judgment. It is important to be made of the right stuff to be effective in what we want to achieve in life. I don't think we necessarily need to be born with the right stuff, it's more that we stuff ourselves rightly and know that the demeanor we choose will lead to our success or our failure. A helpful quality for a student to possess for the stuffing I am speaking of is to be able to surrender to the processes of learning.

The way you go about developing your talent is critical. The best way is to go to the source for the knowledge you wish to obtain, whatever the source, whether it be a person or a horse, nature itself or a good book. When you have found that source, it is up to you to find the hidden lessons from your own perception. If you don't have the ability to find the hidden lessons, know they will come anyway.

My dad gave me the basics of how to ride. When my horse and I were a complete match, my dad felt that it was safe to ride by myself. I was then left alone to enjoy riding my horse, Mustang. I looked for instruction only when my experience and relationship with Mustang was not working for me. This lack of instruction and freedom gave me the invaluable trial and error part of my education. I believe trial and error many times is the missing ingredient with many people learning horsemanship. The errors I experienced with Mustang made me humble enough to listen to my mentors with the appropriate respect when I asked for their help. Trial and error is very important to seasoning communication skills. From being left on my own I developed better horsemanship skills. I was never afraid to experiment and always cautious not to get the horse

or myself hurt. Anything I did with a horse, I would run the consequences through my head before I put my plan into action, and I
always had another plan of action I knew would work for me if my
plan of action failed. The importance of failure is that it will guide
you to seek the kind of help that will really empower you.

When my skill had matured to allow me to handle dangerous
behavior in horses, the more I worked with horses that could hurt
me, the more it developed my reason and intuition. Reasoning and
intuition are also part of the stuffing I spoke of earlier. Developing
horsemanship is slow going and takes place in stages.

Each chapter in the book focuses on the perceptions that brought
me to my greatest successes. Having the right perception is the key
to achieving a great relationship with horses. The paramount rule
in relating to horses is to create harmony through your communication; in that moment, you have an opportunity to lead.

One of the perceptions that empowered me to my most important discovery of horse communication was that if I was respectful
and went to a herd of wild horses with my desire, they would feel
a need to teach me their ways and language. I went to the horses
knowing fully that I knew nothing. My cup was empty. That was
easy for me because when I first joined a herd of wild horses, I
knew nothing. Luckily, I realized that the reason I gained knowledge came from my understanding that I knew nothing. Today it
is the place I still work from because it has so many benefits for
learning and creating. I try always to stay the student. By staying the
student, life is exciting and I am at my greatest ability. The world is
full of teachers, and everyone loves a student.

The last advice I have to offer is to pick an experience you wish to
have with horses that is uplifting. I see so many riders not knowing
that the negative behavior they experience with their horse does
not have to be like that. Most bad times with horses are either from
picking the wrong horse (whether it be from being over mounted
or mismatched) or choosing a horse that does not fit the purpose
you have intended to fit. It is important to understand that it is
your responsibility to set up circumstances to get your horse to
respond the way you would like him to respond.

Enjoying the process is the best way to win the cooperation of
your horse. It is all about focusing on the ease of getting what you
want. Getting what you want feels really good. Like when your

horse steps into a trailer without a struggle or gives you a flying lead change the first time you ask for one and it feels as smooth as butter. Or when you are riding your horse to music and you can feel his body performing to the rhythm of the music and at the same time he seems to be performing from your thoughts and feelings.

When you and your horse can get lost in a world of dance, this is the art of horsemanship. This is when it is totally humane to ask your horse to perform for you at the top of his ability because he is enjoying his performance. You have increased his life's experiences.

It is important to have what you want; anything is possible that connects you to your passion and rattles you to your bones and sets your spirit free! From this place of being is where creative expression abounds.

"The creative is the place where no one else has been; you have to leave the city of your comfort and go into the wilderness of your intuition. You can't get there by bus; only hard work and risk and by not quite knowing what you are doing. What you discover will be wonderful. What you discover will be yourself."

When I heard these words recounted by a friend, I felt they were my own, but I must admit they are the words of Allan Alda.

I set the stories up so that your own perception will lead you to the information that you are hoping to find in the same way my perception guided me to what I learned when I joined a herd of horses in the wild as a young child. As you develop your understanding, the book will offer more and more information and insight. I meant *Naked Liberty* to be a reference book that can be referred to over the course of a lifetime in relating with and training of horses.

Presenting my adventure stories in the unknown world of nature, I intended to help the reader get in touch with their instinctive genius and problem solving skills through reading about my trial and error approach developing acceptance of wild horses through learning their language and pecking order rituals.

On your journey in your relationship with horses, may you find your true bliss that your horse can enjoy with you. Horses have taken people for centuries to new lands and higher values. Horses have a way of opening our eyes to see the connection in all things from our efforts to become better horsemen. Horses are the gatekeepers to human's higher self. For centuries small men have tried to shape and control and domesticate their spirit. It is not about shaping the horse. It is about shaping ourselves worthy enough to be carried not by their submission but by their spirit and will. Horses should be ridden like a surfer rides a wave. The surfer does not force or change the wave. The surfer learns how to ride. The greatest horsemen are the ones who know that the horse's spirit should not be diminished. A great horseman steps into the horse's world and gains a horse's respect and gets the horse to accept his leadership on the horse's terms, not on his. Great horsemen ride in partnership with their horse. The best way to develop leadership ability is to follow the golden rule of ethics: If you create harmony through communication, in that moment you have an opportunity to lead.

It would be my pleasure if *Naked Liberty* increases the partnership between you and your horse and develops your horsemanship, leadership and communication. Enjoy!!

Carolyn Resnick

Book One

Guided by Passion

Carolyn Resnick

Introduction

The following poem helped me outline my book. It kept me on my path of what I was willing to share. I wrote the book passionately. In this way, creating the book was clearly as enjoyable to me as my experience in nature and possibly as important.

A Drink from the Water's Edge

There is mayhem in the street.
Traffic is stopped.
There is spirit in the wind.
People are watching.
Horses are running everywhere,
flared nostrils, white-eyed, bellies heaving bellowed cries,
pavement lifted in the air like confetti as they storm the town
looking for their freedom.
Searching, knowing it is somewhere
as independence leads their way.
My dream feels and hears,
but manifests only in metaphors
until the horses are heard, liberated and honored.
Pine trees, horses, seasons, waterways, lakes and oceans,
community sharing the poetry of the spirit of the wild horses,
broken from chains to speak their minds and be heard.
Horses speak to me of unity, community, totality,
the understanding of individual rights
and when community needs should come first.
My desire clearly gives birth to it all

and explodes from the inside out,
from waiting until it is ripe,
or sung out in a song that echoes forever
in the hoof beats in the face of need.
And so, it was a passion greater than a month
or a lifetime,
more like always.
Horses connect to a rhythm seen and felt and shared
between the breezes, the predators, the love of the breathing earth
and me.
Nostrils guide the way of speech
never disturbing the gap
and yet we speak as freely as the wind will allow.
Should I never forget a drink shared at the water's edge
with eyes glued on each other because we both knew
it tasted better that way.
Let me gaze into your eyes
as I sip water
that pulls and rushes between my lips,
the same as yours,
like I have heard Native Americans share blood cut
from the arm for the ceremony
of brotherhood, that we are one.
You ask me to tell you about horses.
Come with me,
and I will share with you my dreams,
but don't expect to rip my story from me
without a drink together first
from the water's edge.

I am not sure what it was about horses that first struck me: the
sound of their hooves on pavement, their pure potential for flight,
or that they would let me ride them. Whatever it was, it was a
sensuous and spiritual draw. I must have fallen in love with horses
hundreds of times for all different reasons, from their beauty and
spirit to the smell of their bodies that permeated my clothing after
a long ride. Maybe it was a feeling of beauty that came from inside,
a perception of life they held that was truly beautiful, an aura that I
could feel just by being in the same space with them. It was an im-

mediate attraction that first took place for me as a small child.

One day at home, I heard hoofbeats.

"What is that sound?" I asked.

My mother lifted me up to a window and told me, "It is the sound of the horses' hooves on the street." "Horses!" I repeated over and over again. I tried to reach with my arms to be closer. And that is the way it has been from that day forward.

Everything changed for me. I listened differently. I felt differently. I behaved toward everything differently. Horses gave a sense of importance to everything, yet it wasn't until thirty years later that I was able to share my experiences with anyone. It took me that long to figure out how to put what I had discovered into words. I found a world that humans are not aware of, where language has no words.

I learned to look at the world through the eyes of a horse. I could see the connection between what I was looking at and myself. It was a miraculous awakening. I shared only the essence of life. For me, it was a totally separate experience in unity.

Horses introduced me to the web of nature as an ongoing experience. I was introduced to simple everyday interactions in the pastoral scenes of horses as I gazed often at their back-lit manes mapping the direction of the wind, while being invited to listen to something, I knew not what, from a single, cocked ear. I could feel nature living right up to the silhouetted edge of my own existence from watching horses living out their simple daily habits. It was no time at all until I discovered that every new horse I met spoke to me through a language we both understood but that neither of us had ever used before.

Some people may remember an article about a kitten that accidentally got into a bear's cage while the bear was eating chicken. The kitten was hungry and walked right up to the bear and begged with a simple meow. The bear reached down into the bucket, drew out some food and gave it to the kitten. They have been fast friends since that moment of unexplainable communication. This is the same communication I share with horses.

Through this type of kindred spirit, horses have brought me to know myself. One gift I received from horses is the ability to use an instinct I was born with to communicate with them through a magical connection we share. This connection comes naturally to almost all animals, some adults and many children. Horses brought me to my passion and true nature, or my "true north." I like to refer to this way of communicating as a "universal language," one that all animals understand.

I think what Kipling wrote about in *The Jungle Book* when he referred to keeping the jungle law, living always for the community good, is that there is an ability to communicate with all things. When the jungle law is honored, it creates harmonious acts without resistance. When humans remember to keep the sense of community in the act of communication, rapport is the result.

I have the idea that horses are born with an instinct to be ridden. We are born with an instinct to ride them. I came to this possibly outlandish idea after discovering that wild horses in a natural herd would spontaneously allow me onto their backs. Whatever the conditions necessary for the phenomenon to occur between my world and theirs, this was the way horses chose to respond to me.

In my search for a method of training that horses find enjoyable, I developed a connection with horses that I refer to today as a magnetic connection. I believe this connection is the same one that herd animals use to communicate with each other when the herd becomes united in a "one-mind consciousness."

This connection is seen in a stampede of wild horses or in a large school of fish in unison escaping an attack. This connection unifies direction and movement and is important in training horses because you can use it as a system of communication. It will make it easier to direct your horse using fewer aids. The aids you use will be almost imperceptible, and your horse's performance will be superior.

This bond has served me in many forms of horsemanship, from dressage to Western reining horses, from English pleasure horses to Western pleasure horses, from gaited horses to fine harness horses. I think craft and formula are important in horsemanship, but the key is how much the horse is willing to give to the performance. I believe that the relationship between trainer and horse must spring from likeability, companion energy and magnetism. A champion performance occurs when it is the horse's idea to perform, when he believes the show is held purely for his fancy and when rider and horse become one entity, like a centaur. Behind the championship performance is the unbridled spirit.

I like to think of the art of horsemanship as a formula that can be applied with the least amount of effort. If a horse can feel a fly, he can feel an aid of the same lightness and perform happily. For a horse to be this sensitive to human needs, he must have a great desire to perform. The highest desire in all horses is companionship. No horse should be made to perform. We must seek his permission and fulfill his requirement for companionship.

My relationship with horses as a child and my struggle to understand this magical connection between their world and mine is my own story.

This love affair with horses is part and parcel of my method of communication. My connection with horses is like the connection shared between twins. This intense energy field that binds us together is similar to the magnetism migrating geese share in the unity of flight. The horse becomes a mirrored reflection of my movement. When we share this connection, the horse feels a sense of well-being. This sense of well-being creates his need to follow my lead, together in the moment, one movement inventing another. I am in the horse's world and he is in mine.

Carolyn Resnick

Book Two

Memoirs of My
Childhood

Carolyn Resnick

Chapter I

In The Beginning

The Bond Has Its Own Language

Looking back to my childhood is like looking at a 1000-piece puzzle laid out separately on a table, challenging me to piece together the picture but much harder because so many of my memories are forgotten through the rivers of time. The experiences that I had as a child with horses began before my first memory. My first memory of horses was when I heard the sound of hooves on the street during a parade. There were elephants, lions and tigers, clowns, floats, decorated bicycles and circus wagons. An old calliope was huffing and puffing, spitting out carousel music into the air. At the same time, I could hear music and drums of a marching band. But the sound that stood out most to me, was the sound of the horses' hooves on the street. I was very young, still a toddler.

My mother told me that I was already crazy about horses before the parade. The first time she put me on a horse I was just old enough to sit up on my own. Because of my reaction she knew that my connection with horses was natural. She told me that when the horse was walking, my body naturally joined the rhythm of the horse and when the horse stopped, I sat still for a moment then began the walking rhythm in an attempt to influence the horse to continue walking.

So I guess I can say that my relationship with horses began from a rhythm that drew me to horses and a rhythm that came naturally as a way to communicate when I rode.

The time in history that I grew up, the path I chose to follow and the horses that I got to know along the way were the greatest influences in my childhood. It was the first experiences with each horse that shaped the opinions I have today. There was Mustang,

Strawberry, Sunnyboy, Babe, Flashlight, Lover, Sweetypie, Chubbs
Melody, Mustano, Moonlight, Sagebrush, all the horses I got to
know around Hercky Creek, and the horses I had in training and
the countless horses in between. Maybe it wasn't in that order and
maybe they weren't the biggest influence in my life, but surely they
were the beginning.

I grew up in the Coachella Valley desert of Southern California in
the days of no fences. Along with horses, I had a love of nature and
the environment. Horses took me on journeys that were certainly
easier than on foot, especially traveling through the sandy desert.
I would like to recall my memories by starting with Strawberry or
Mustang but what brings back my memories with greatest clarity
are the places we traveled together.

The places we traveled were in the desert and so I must speak of
the desert. The desert returns me to my origin. As I piece together the
jigsaw puzzle of my memories, a panoramic view of the hot sands of
the Coachella Valley appears to me more real than the experience.

There are many kinds of deserts that existed in the Coachella
Valley: high deserts, low deserts, deserts of chaparral and cactus,
deserts of nothing but sand and occasional oases and a myriad of
others; my passion was to see them all on the back of my horse.

A common theme in the desert is a lack of rain on a floor of sand
as far as the eye can see. Oases are usually only imaginary. There are
virtually no lakes or streams. The desert I grew up in unites all who
live there as everyone seeks refuge from the harsh conditions. Resting in shade was a welcome refuge. Everyone – men, women and
children and all animals – stopped what they were doing in the heat
of the day and went about finding a comfortable place to pass the
time, waiting for the weather to cool off.

Shade was a gift. Just to lie limp, to float in a hammock, to dream
of paradise, to feel something besides discomfort from the summer
sun was a blessing.

The desert taught me how to feel, first from the discomfort and
then from the relief. From the relief there is an understanding of
meditation. That space that comes between thoughts until thoughts
disappear and are replaced by quiet solitude. In that space of
suspended thought and appreciation for the smallest pleasures, in
those moments I gained a perception of nature that connected me
to the elements and an understanding of the animal mind. It was

odd that in the heat with all its discomforts, I experienced a pure joy. I remember every fiber of my existence was focused on waiting for a breeze or some sort of relief. The heat brought my positive thinking to its highest ability and created a kind of euphoria through the suffering.

It was hard to be alone in the desert. The sun was my constant companion. All metal was a first-degree burn looking to happen. Jewelry, doorknobs, any place you sat down that was in the sun – all had the potential to burn. Leather inside a car could burn you through your clothing. Bicycle handlebars or nails in a bench could cause anyone to scream out in surprised anguish.

Growing up in all of this heat seemed natural to me from early childhood. Facing the summer heat and finding a kind of pleasure in it, I developed an extreme tolerance for the sun. As long as I had my horses and my tolerance for the heat, the desert became my playground.

The greatest part of my education with horses came from the ranch we moved to when I was eight years old, and then later from the wild horses around Garner Valley in the mountains above the town of Indio.

On the days I rode, I would ride across the desert as far as I could and still be back home by sundown. In the desert's freedom, I found there were laws to be followed to stay safe and what could happen for not being alert to possible danger. Within the matrix of law, order and freedom there is a magical chain of communication that connects all desert creatures. From having to comply to these laws of survival and by knowing the desert intimately, a universal language is gained.

On the days I did not ride, I spent many hours studying our horses' herd behavior to learn as much as I could about the basic behavior of horses and how to communicate with them in a natural herd society. I joined them when they were grazing on my family's forty acre ranch. Because we irrigated, there were many grazing opportunities around the property for the horses. Beyond those sixty acres there was only sand and a few dead, dried up bushes here and there. Because the ranch was unfenced, sometimes the horses would leave. On these excursions, the horses and I found a freedom in companionship to roam and interact without restraint. I experienced the desert like animals experience their everyday existence. Horses seemed to recognize and accept me as one of them. I joined them on foot or climbed onto their backs when they were roaming freely. I felt that horses were family, not that they were a part of my human family but I saw myself as part of their family.

Before the Coachella Valley aqueduct, ranches were sparsely scattered across the valley. Ownership of territory was determined by who got there first. Water was enough to designate settlement. People settled where water could be found underground through well drilling. My grandfather was one of the first welldrillers in the valley.

There was an aura left behind from these first settlers, a freedom in the forties and fifties that went unnoticed and now is lost forever. There was an unexplainable freedom when boundaries were flexible. There was no need to know right where your property line was. There was friendship and understanding between neighbors and residents. When rapport was the common condition, there was no need for fences. My relationship with animals was developed from the freedom that existed in that time in history.

When I grew up, my family never locked the house or removed the key from our car, and everyone was my friend unless they proved otherwise. I was always ready to repair a relationship because companionship was as precious as water.

There was nothing on the land for livestock to graze upon if one did not irrigate. Ranchers who had farm animals kept only a few because feed was expensive. Since there was no food or water anywhere else, the animals clearly understood the importance of humans. This caused them to trust people completely. Their trust played a major part in my understanding horses.

During the day, our animals were free to roam around. Animals and people shared common ground around the barn site. We did not need fencing to keep animals at home because the only place they could get food and water was in the barn. If they wandered off, they would be back when it was time to eat or drink. At night they were caught up and put into corrals, coops and pens close to the barn for protection from predators and theft.

Pasture fencing and ownership fencing was uncommon. The Catron family was the first I heard of to put in pasture fencing in the valley. The Kennedy family was next, but by then I was already half grown.

Growing up with horses in a fenceless environment was important to my growth in horsemanship, especially when it came time to catch the horse I wanted to ride.

To catch a horse or to train a horse without the help of a fence took a lot of know how. The horses all knew that if they didn't want to be caught, they could run away. They knew that if they bucked me off, they had plainly told me to watch my step. We were on equal ground. At the beginning of each day, the bond with the horses was my only connection. There was a code I had to follow because the desert and the horses held me to it.

The desert's large spaces and lack of population influenced my need for companionship. Friendship became my highest priority. Over time, I rode in partnership through a myriad of deserts. My horses showed me that they were nature lovers who learned to live their lives in the harmony of diversity.

What I discovered was a magnetic connection, maybe the formula that makes living things live. From this connection I developed an understanding of psychic energy that is important for communication.

My horses and I discovered a perception of language that was different than a world of words. I discovered body language, expressions and primitive sounds. By interacting with horses in the desert, sharing their customs and communicating with them in their own language, I found horses had a natural desire to be ridden without training if you developed a friendship with them. This was important for me to learn because I wanted to believe that the horse enjoyed taking me on a ride as much as I enjoyed riding. In my search to understand how horses felt about being ridden, I soon became aware that the perception and behavior of horses could be changed through the bond I developed with them.

In the community I shared with my horses, in their world and family, I discovered that the art of horsemanship has little to do with horse training and everything to do with communication and friendship. The highest form of communication occurs when there is a bond in the moment of the request. In the bond of true friendship, there is an ebb and flow like the tide. When the request happens in the flow, instead of the ebb, true communication occurs.

I learned to communicate when the bond was the strongest between us. It is the kind of communication that is above abuse and tenderness. It is another world, space and time. The highest form of horsemanship comes from a communication of leadership when the horse feels the bond is present from the first to the last interaction.

Fitting memories together like a jigsaw puzzle came to me with missing pieces, but what I wanted to recall is complete. From my first ride that my mother recounted to me, to my first memory of her lifting me up to the window to see the horses prancing in the parade, to the adventures with my horses in the desert, I can see clearly how my roots were formed. From those roots I discovered that in the moment of the bond, the bond has its own language.

Chapter II

National Champion Everything

My First Teacher

My early childhood was shaped before we had air-conditioning and television. I grew up in the days of iceboxes and horse-drawn ice wagons, milkmen with milk and eggs, and hobos looking for work at your back door. During the forties, mothers were home and fathers were at work. It was a slower time. A time when Monday was washing and Tuesday was ironing.

One of my earliest memories is of the wash hanging on the clothesline, soaking up the fresh smell of the outdoors, and of the laundry being sprinkled with water flung from fingertips dipped into a bowl and rolled up into a towel to set until uniformly damp for ironing. This was a chore that had to be done with a measure of speed and accuracy to feel a sense of pride in the task and in being a proper caretaker. Neighbors, family, in-laws and friends scrutinized all chores. How well you did your chores determined your worth as a housewife and mother. Everyone had chores, responsibilities, hobbies and children played throughout the neighborhood freely, without fear.

Indio was a small town in the desert with a population of no more than 1500. We lived in the middle of town next door to my dad's blacksmith shop. Our family name was White. On the other side of our house was my grandmother's house. Across the street was the Nazarene church and across from it was the Methodist church. Many Sundays I watched the hustle and bustle of the congregations as they filed into the churches. In those days everyone dressed up and women wore fancy hats. I dressed up every Sunday whether I went to church or not.

The center of town was only two blocks away. Business and residences intermingled around the railroad station. Indio came into being because of the railroad. The train stopped there to pick up water before heading up the San Bernardino grade to Los Angeles.

Indio was an attractive village stuck smack dab in the middle of a desert in Southern California. The town was landscaped with palm trees and orange trees. Because of the desert desolation surrounding the town of Indio, residents took great pride in developing beautiful cottage gardens. Most of the homes were bungalows or early mission-style cottages. All the homes had front and back porches with an unattached garage on the side of the house. White picket fences lined the sidewalks. One block past town there was no sign of civilization, just desert, a desert of grayish white sand for miles in every direction. In the far horizon, the San Jacinto Mountains rose ten thousand feet above sea level. It could be 100 degrees in town and at the same time we could see snowcapped mountains in the distance.

Telephones had party lines and it took an operator to connect your call. Picking up the phone, one could listen to someone else's conversation and no one objected if the third party joined in. Neighbors would busy themselves talking about the new stop sign and be amazed and pleased with any signs of growth in town. Everyone went to town hall meetings. All in all, it seemed to me that town growth and progress was the major focus of the people who lived there.

Influenced by the talk about Indio and its growth, I spent much time investigating the neighborhood, watching for new construction and enjoying my neighbor's cottage gardens.

Adults loved children and neighbors had a part in raising us. Indio was an extended family. Wherever we were, the neighbors would keep an eye on us. Between our horse games and hopscotch, we would hang out in the afternoon waiting for the Good Humor ice cream truck and its jingle, which could be heard two blocks away. Ice cream in the desert was a special treat.

It was unique having horses in the middle of town. We kept our horses at my dad's blacksmith shop. My family for generations had kept horses. Both of my grandfathers trained draft horses. My dad's father trained teams of horses for pulling and had trained horses that put up the tents for Barnum and Bailey Circuses.

No one in town minded that we had horses. We could ride right through town and into the desert and anywhere we wanted. I can't remember much about those rides because I was young, but I do recall my first horse and how I felt about him.

His name was Strawberry. Over twenty years old, he was a deep-eyed, retired plow horse. Usually a plow horse is a draft horse, but Strawberry resembled a mustang. He was a strawberry roan and stood about fifteen hands. He had an exaggerated Roman nose. He was not much to look at because of his age and his bony profile. I thought he was beautiful and have been partial to Roman-nosed horses ever since. Many people remarked that his color had special qualities; they said strawberry roans were different than all other horses. I am glad they didn't point out his moth-eaten appearance and stuck to his positive personality traits.

My first teacher in horsemanship, outside our family, was a man who worked in my father's blacksmith shop. He also worked for Barnum and Bailey Circus in the summertime. Everyone called him Long Line because he was also a telephone lineman. I always thought he was called Long Line because of the tall tales he told any time someone stopped long enough to listen.

Long Line was usually the reason I got to go riding. My parents looked at Long Line as my nanny; I looked at him as my ticket to ride. He taught me riding, but not with the typical "heels down and sit up straight" talk of the classical approach with beginners. Long Line taught by creating fantasy games from the stories he shared with me of his circus life with horses and elephants. He always was careful to add that Strawberry was the best of all of the horses he had ever run across. Someday, he said, we would go to the grand nationals and show the world what a great horse Strawberry was by winning National Champion Everything.

Much to my joy, we played the same game for a couple of years. I would pretend to be Strawberry at a horse show and Long Line was the announcer and judge. He had a loud barker's voice and announced the classes one by one as if it were the greatest show on earth. He described every imaginary horse in detail as it entered the arena. He said something like, "And all the way from Detroit, the beautiful grand champion daughter from the Royal Dutch line 'Regional King,' last year's winner of the Emerald Cup Award, the beautiful palomino mare Lady Slipper, ridden by Dan Chapman." Then he cupped his hands together and blew a breath into them, sounding like an audience applauding her entrance.

I stayed waiting my turn in total suspense while he announced all my competition. Each description was more colorful than the next. I got so scared, I almost did not want to compete. But I stayed focused and told myself that I could do it. I knew I could. Then a shiver ran down my back as he said, "And last, but not least, all the way from Indio, California, a surprise entry, and a new challenger on the scene. Let's give them a hand, ladies and gentlemen – Strawberry, ridden by Carolyn White!"

I entered the arena with the most beautiful trot I could muster. For the next ten to fifteen minutes, Long Line proceeded to almost maniacally work me to my fullest physical capacity. He barked out requests for walk, trot and canter, in both directions of the arena. Sometimes I performed over a jump course built from household objects and ranch supplies: brooms, chairs, old tools, empty boxes and bales of hay. We even built a water jump out of my plastic wading pool – it was my favorite jump. For the driving classes, I dragged a couple of bamboo sticks behind me so I could feel the shafts against my body as I went into the turns. I learned how much effort a horse must expend to perform by how much effort it took to keep my prancing up at the end of my performance.

When Long Line thought I'd had enough, he'd call me into the center of the arena for the last inspection of the judging. I stood very still and waited patiently, maybe pawing the ground a time or two, while Long Line wandered about comparing all the other horses and me. My heart was in my throat as he announced the winners, starting with the fifth place, then fourth.... I stood wondering if I had a chance at all or possibly if I had won the class. Then he'd announce the first place award. That is what I always won, but every time the suspense would build and I was always surprised.

On days when Long Line was not available and I was left to entertain myself, the only thing I could do was stand outside and look into the paddock housing Strawberry. I developed a large imagination from the stories Long Line and I had made up about Strawberry's greatness, so time on my hands became a playground for my mind.

In my four-year-old world before schooling, I could spend all day at home playing with, or watching, or riding Strawberry. One afternoon, my mother said it would be all right to play with Strawberry in the back yard while she watched me from the kitchen window. Usually I was only allowed to watch my horse in his paddock when Long Line had other chores.

On that day, it was as though fate was arranged for me. Even before I could lead him on a rope, I had a playmate. I could play with him all day long. Wherever he went, I followed, much like a baby duckling just hatched will follow anything that moves and declare it "mother." I followed him, fascinated by every bit of grass he took. I lay down next to him and he ate all around my body. By the end of the day, my mother told me she looked out the kitchen window and saw me hanging onto Strawberry's tail while he pulled me across the yard looking for pieces of grass he might have missed earlier.

I learned how to communicate with my horse and problem solve, even finding ways onto his back. I would crawl into a tree and jump onto him. Or I'd crawl over his head and onto his neck while he was grazing and wait for the moment he would raise his head, then slide onto his back. Looking back at these moments, I realize that not enough can be said for older horses and their contribution to first-time horse owners, especially children, in learning horsemanship.

The most important aspect of my relationship with Strawberry was the strong bond we formed in that backyard. He was my first impression of a horse and I measure all horses by the standard he set. I expect all horses to have his best traits. I believe there is a strawberry roan in every horse I meet. I just have to wait a little longer in some cases for my old horse to arrive. I believe Strawberry's trustworthiness and age inspired my courage and bravery. I strongly recommend an older horse for a first-time owner. The world of horses is best shared with a deep-eyed horse.

Carolyn Resnick

Chapter III

Humility

Most of the horse community in Indio spent weekends at the Sheriff's Posse Rodeo Grounds. In those days, many of my friends' fathers were sheriffs, and so was my dad. They were as important to us as the President of the United States. I looked at my father as being a "real cowboy" like Roy Rogers. He sometimes rode my mother's horse, a palomino just like Roy's.

On one of those weekends at the rodeo grounds, some friends asked my father if I could help them straighten out a naughty pony named Pepper. They had owned the pony for six months and said the pony had turned vicious. No one could do a thing with him. Ponies are very smart and they felt that if an adult fixed the pony, it would still not be right for children to ride. Since I had a way with horses and he was a little small for an adult to ride, I was chosen for the task.

Until then, I had known only our horses. At seven years old, I had acquired a reputation as the girl who talked to horses but not because I had achieved any great success with a difficult horse. I acquired this reputation because I did indeed talk to my horse and he did what I told him; this amazed the adult community.

My father thought Pepper would be a good project to develop my horsemanship skills. He felt that Pepper would challenge me but not be so challenging that I would get hurt.

Pepper was a child's dream come true. He was the shiny black pony a child longs to receive on Christmas day. I looked forward to his arrival, fixed his bed, told Strawberry of this new friend who would be arriving soon. I knew Pepper was mean, but I didn't think he would be mean to me. The kids who had him were mean to everyone, so I didn't blame the pony for his behavior. And I had my ace in the hole: Strawberry was going to inform Pepper what a nice place he'd come to and what a good little girl I was.

When Pepper arrived, I watched him back out of the trailer – small, black and beautiful. I spent time with him before I climbed on his back, and he was indeed a nice individual. He led, tied and saddled easily. When the owners saw how he reacted in my charge, they were very impressed.

After they left and when no one was around, I got on his back. I was sure that he was sweet and would do nothing unusual. Boy, was I wrong! He started out just fine and walked along like he was having the time of his life. And I was, too, because I had never ridden a pony before and it was fun being on such a tiny thing. After all, what could he do to me?

I rode him for about five minutes and he behaved perfectly. He walked, he trotted and he cantered. He did everything I asked … until we rode onto a vacant lot with a few trees. Pepper grabbed the bit, bolted and started running away with me. From time to time he'd stop to rub my legs against a tree as hard as he could, tearing my clothes until I was bloody. I couldn't get off him because he ran from tree to tree, and when he stopped, he pinned me against another tree. Finally, he made a mistake. There was enough distance between trees and I was able to bail.

It was quite a shock. Horses had only shown me love and fair play up until then. I had been raised to believe that if a horse did something wrong, it was my fault. As I sat on our porch turning black and blue and crying from hurt feelings and missing skin, I tried to figure out what caused his reaction. I couldn't think of anything I had done wrong, except maybe coveting my neighbor's goods – I was secretly hoping I would be able to keep Pepper.

After a while, the pain went away and I started looking forward to riding Pepper again. I planned to ride him where there was nothing he could rub me off against and where I'd have plenty of chance to get off if he decided to head for dangerous ground. However, before I rode him again, my mother made arrangements to get some help from a top cowboy in our town, Abe Abersald. His name alone spoke to me of a man with a purpose. Abe rode bucking horses in the rodeo. He was afraid of nothing. He told my mother that I should bring Pepper over to his ranch and he would fix that pony for sure.

After my accident, Pepper's owners said I could keep him forever. They did not want him back. I had become the proud owner of the pony of my dreams. Even after what Pepper had done to me, I still loved him. I knew that, with time, I could get him to behave – but first, it was Abe's turn. Maybe he could teach Pepper a lesson. Abe said that Pepper would probably not try anything with him, because Abe knew what he was doing.

It was a sunny morning and very still when I arrived with Pepper, whom I had ridden bareback all the way over to Abe's house. I got down and Abe saddled Pepper and got on him in a huge field enclosed by barbed wire. Pepper wasted no time in showing his opinion of Abe. I learned that day how well I had actually been getting along with Pepper. The treatment Pepper had given me was a show of affection compared to what he did to Abe.

Pepper bucked, leaped, reared, went over backwards pinning Abe under him and rolled to free himself. He threw Abe off several times – Abe, the rodeo king, the man who knew what he was doing! For a decisive stroke, Pepper ran over to the barbed wire fence and pitched Abe onto the top wire. Abe had to go to the doctor for stitches. What an experience! Every time Abe came off Pepper's back, he acted as if it was just a freak accident or as if it hadn't really happened and got right back on. Pepper evidently knew about barbed wire and did not try to rub himself against it. Every time Abe got back on, Pepper had a new way of arranging Abe's dismount. Pepper's strategy worked. Abe never wanted to see Pepper again.

I started to realize Pepper did like me. He had never bucked once with me. While his mind was still on Abe, I got on his back and rode home through the desert where there were no trees or fences. He was a good boy with me. All the way home, I could hear him in my mind, cussing out Abe.

I would like to say everything went smoothly after that, but it didn't. He was my first teacher in the art of communication with difficult horses and ponies. I had to have a great imagination to look past the whuppin' Pepper had just given Abe and see the good, kind, sweet pony that was not visible that day. With advice from my parents and through a process of trial and error, I learned rules for getting the job done with a horse that had different opinions from my own. I still use these rules today.

What Pepper taught me is never to assume that any animal you don't know is going to respond in a certain manner toward you, no matter how strongly you believe it. All horses are individuals. The way a horse responds toward one person is not necessarily how he will respond to someone else; the way a horse responds one day is not necessarily how he will respond the next. If I had known more about Pepper's personality, I could have handled him better.

Pepper was a pony that didn't like to be told what to do. He liked to be asked. The reason he rubbed me off on the trees was that he felt that our relationship was going too quickly for me to be so demanding. He put a stop to it, without anger. If I had asked less of him and put him up sooner, he would have been fine. At the Abersold ranch, Abe picked a fight with Pepper and Pepper obliged him. The bucking scene between Abe and Pepper showed me that force was not the solution. Most accidents happen from a lack of communication and new relationships are where the accident is most likely to happen.

I use Pepper's lesson today. When a horse comes to me for training, I wait a few days for him to settle in and get to know me and for me to get to know him. It is the first step of my method of training horses. What Abe taught me is that there are easier ways to handle horses than fighting their resistance. Sometimes, all a horse has is resistance, and this was where Pepper was heading.

When I started with Pepper, my attention was on my agenda, not on Pepper. I made the mistake of not being in the moment and I needed to see that, in his eyes, he felt pushed. I didn't heed Pepper's warning signs of discontent. He definitely took the reins and headed out to the tree lot. I should have changed his direction or gotten off him. I didn't know him well enough to have saddled him up and asked for walk, trot and canter, all within fifteen minutes, especially since I had been warned. I was in a hurry. I needed to slow down. I was hunting for trouble and trouble I found.

Pepper went through a contrary phase before he started behaving. He did the opposite of whatever I asked. If I kicked him, he stopped. If I asked him to turn right, he turned left. I learned that if I wanted to turn left, I had to ask him to turn right. If I wanted to go, I pulled back on the reins. I never punished him. I waited until he was settled, then asked again.

Pepper finally figured out that I was onto him and using his reactions to get what I wanted. That's when he turned sweet and willing. I am not sure why, but that is the way horses and ponies are, if given half a chance.

On the Path to Horsemanship

Compliments of Pepper the Pony

When you are in the company of your horse, he should have your full attention. A horse feels more secure with a rider who manages, directs and monitors his flexible nature. A person that is most aware of his horse at every moment has the most dependable horse.

Let the moment guide you in your training decisions.

Follow safety rules at all times.

Notice your horse's responses – desirable and undesirable

When correcting your horse's behavior, never ask for anything you are not qualified or experienced enough to accomplish.

Enjoy every interaction with your horse as a lesson in relationship.

Focus on your horse's successes, not on his failures.

Never be in a hurry.

When things get tough, go back to something that he is willing to do and start over again. No matter how challenging your relationship, you can go back to this seed as your starting point.

Imagination is the key to finding solutions.

It is your job to keep your horse in a good mood or to create the proper mood before you ask him to perform for you.

A good horseman is a person that depends on his ability to lead rather than upon the benevolence of his horse.

Chapter IV

Mustang

In the Days of No Fences

Around the age of 8, when I was in elementary school, my parents realized their dream of owning a ranch and purchased about forty acres a mile and a half outside of Indio. When we moved to the ranch, we left the community of Indio and our friends and neighbors to live as ranchers, isolated from town and community. No longer could I run over to a friend's house whenever I wanted. No longer could I walk the neighborhood looking for children to play with. At the time, I didn't sense my loss of community and friends because I was too excited about moving onto a real ranch in the desert. I was going to be able to ride whenever and wherever I wanted. I was going to experience pure freedom.

My mother had prepared me for our move. She shared her love for the desert with me. She also read many stories including "Aladdin's Lamp," "Princess Scheherazade," "Drinkers of the Wind" and "Ali Baba and the Forty Thieves." These stories led me to believe that there was real magic in the desert that existed nowhere else.

I loved the desert's harshness, isolation and freedom. Not only would I be able to ride alone in nature, I would be able to find the wild animals of the desert and learn how to communicate with them. I was impressed with their ability to stay alive in such harsh conditions. The desert creatures were evolutionary wonders created by arid conditions.

The hot weather and relentless, clear blue skies had left everything scalding. Over time evolution has given desert creatures garments of scales, shells, needles and made their bodies flat and tough so they can wedge under rocks, cactus and sand to avoid death from the afternoon sun.

I honored these creatures and respected them for being able
to survive. Not only did they survive, I could see that they really
enjoyed their lives and were sensitive to subtle pleasures like a cool
breeze or shade in the afternoon. They actually enjoyed these moments and their attitude taught me how to enjoy things that people
overlook or take for granted. Watching a cottontail rabbit nibbling
on a blade of grass, I could see a kind of rapture in his experience,
a rapture that fascinated me. Animals are truly in love with the
moment, always curious and grateful for the smallest rewards. I did
not accept the idea that their joyful state of being was due to their
lower intelligence. I chose to enjoy the same state of being so that I,
too, could get lost in the rapture myself. I developed a heightened
awareness of my surroundings and found that pleasure in everyday
activities became my greatest focus and reward. In this state, the
sound of morning songbirds became as thrilling to me as the blade
of grass was to the cottontail rabbit.

The desert has a peculiar cleanliness. In the mornings, the air has
a fresh aroma of sage and other desert plants. The sky and land are
veiled in pastel shades of rainbow colors. The desert magnified my
appreciation for the beauty and the uniqueness of all things. All
who survive in the desert develop a mind for details, and that is
a blessing because without the appreciation for details, the desert
would not be comfortable or rewarding.

When we moved to the ranch, my dad bought me a new horse to
replace Strawberry. Strawberry was over thirty years old and Dad
felt he needed to be retired. I did not believe he was right. Strawberry appeared no worse for the wear to me.

My family explained that Strawberry needed to retire because he
deserved the reward of pasture life until he died. It would be best
for him to retire when he was still sound and able to experience his
retirement in good health. I had not noticed him slowing down. It
was hard for me to part with him. I would no longer be able to see
him everyday as he was retired thirty miles from our home. I was
sad to lose his company, but I came to understand that it was for
the best.

My new horse, Mustang, was better equipped for traveling
through the desert terrain than Strawberry. Mustang was like the
spirit of the wind. He was a wild horse that had been caught in
the San Jacinto Mountains just above the Coachella Valley. Newly

gelded and broken the hard way, he was six years old and had been under saddle for a few short months before my dad purchased him for me. He was still wild by nature and leery of people, and they were leery of him. When I rode him and called him by name, people stepped aside and gave us room.

At first, we kept him in a small corral for fear he would run back to the wild. Unlike a domestic horse, Mustang could have survived without the support of humans. If we had turned him loose then, he would have left the ranch.

Although he permitted me to ride him, it was many months before Mustang grew to like me. But once he liked me, I could depend on his support and friendship more than if he were human. Over time, his love for me grew to such an extent that even though the free-range land where he grew up was just a few days travel from our ranch, he chose to stay when we finally let him run free. He was so devoted to me that if anyone else tried to feed him, he would not eat.

All the cowboys in town agreed that Mustang was quite the looker. Mustang was a blood-bay, just 14.2 hands. He had black legs with four white socks and a blaze that accented his long, chiseled head with large, open nostrils. His top lip was squared and strong and his eyes were large and expressive. He always held them open beyond their natural large size, an indication he was no ordinary horse. When I told strangers that he was a mustang and wild most of his life, no one ever doubted his lineage.

Because I was so enamored with owning a wild mustang, I left his side as little as possible. I spent time just watching him, trying to find what made him different. Many days I watched him dust the desert for hidden grasses. Minutes would go by before he would find a single blade. When he found one, he would snap it off quickly and continue sweeping the desert floor, looking for another blade of grass. Sometimes he would dig up roots and eat parts of them. I had never seen a domestic horse do that.

Mustang's ears were narrow and medium-sized, hooked at the tips. He used his ears as if to show them off, twisting them in a very attractive manner. His ears sat at the very top of his head, close to his poll, while other horses' ears were set much lower and wider, giving them a quiet, sedate appearance. His legs were dry, clean and correct, with perfectly shaped hooves that were hard to trim because of their toughened condition. His body was round and short-coupled, packed with the energy, power and the presence of a stallion. He had been gelded and cut proud, but that was okay; in fact, that was his charm. (Cut proud is a term that means that the operation was not preformed right and the horse is left with the same behavior of a stallion. But the horse is unable to produce offspring.) Although he'd been captured and broken the hard way, he never forgot who he was – the proud leader of a herd of wild horses.

I fondly remember how he would separate his gestures, posing like a statue in stone before bursting out with a prancing stride and blowing nostrils. Even under my control, he would swell with pride when we joined groups of horses and riders. He would call attention to himself by rearing and striking into the air. Here I was, a child of 9 years, feeling as safe as if I were at home on the couch. In all the years I had him, he never bucked me off. He protected me in every way.

His mind was keen, his gaits were smooth. Unlike most horses, Mustang had many speeds of walk, trot and canter. No horse has ever suited me better for comfort. When I rode him, he allowed me to pick the direction I wanted to go as if it were his idea. He raised my awareness of my surroundings and the pleasure we experienced together. He shared his thoughts with me so clearly, I knew what it was to be a horse. Not only did he transport me across the desert of the Coachella Valley, he shared his world of optimistic adventure, caution and the magic to be found in the moment. He taught me to believe that invisibility could be our greatest protection and the power of conduct could gain the respect of anyone we happened to meet. He carried me into the world of natural things and into an understanding of places humans do not go, or even know about.

Mustang often demonstrated his intelligence. He was housed at my family's ranch with a mustang mare. My father bought the mare from a rent string for fifty dollars to keep Mustang company and give us an extra horse for visitors to ride. Her name was Babe. She was a small bay with one white foot and a blaze. About twelve years old, her most notable features were her Roman nose, her bony profile, her herring gut and her desire to run like the wind. She was the safest but most rough-gaited horse on our ranch. She had little personality and showed no opinion or preference for anything, except that she hated horse trailers.

Mustang saw none of these flaws. With Babe, his life on our ranch was complete, until we got so many horses that he had to share both his paddock and Babe with Bryan.

Bryan was a chestnut Belgian workhorse, every bit of 17 hands. Mustang tried to drive Bryan away from Babe, but Bryan was so big, he hardly noticed. Mustang would charge, bite and kick. Bryan, a placid horse by nature, after working all day in the field, didn't seem to care.

Mustang did not give up the fight. Inside the paddock where all three horses were housed, there was a smaller paddock we used only for lay-ups. Mustang worked at the gate to that small paddock until he unlocked it. Then, using skills honed in his days as a wild stallion, he herded Babe into it. Soon Bryan followed the mare inside. Mustang then herded her out, and before Bryan had a chance to follow, Mustang shut the gate and locked it.

This went on every day, but Bryan never learned to stay out of the lay-up paddock. I guess Bryan was just a little slow and Mustang had a great need. I could have fixed that gate, but after all, Mustang wanted some time away from Bryan and I enjoyed watching their antics. It got so that Mustang just had to open the door and Bryan would walk right in with Mustang closing the door behind him.

Mustang helped me realize that what I had been told about a horse's lack of intelligence was wrong. I'm sure this conclusion was reached without spending appropriate time observing and researching the intelligence of horses. I have learned that there is more to instinct than a simple reflex response to environmental stimuli, and far more than mere instinctual behavior originates separately from the conscious mind. I have come to believe that animals possess instinctive reasoning, a natural ability for problem solving that derives from instinct and conscious choice working together.

Mustang embodied these elements with a good sense of self and fair play. He had an understanding of community responsibility and acted on that understanding. After a long bout of locking his rival up, he eventually took pity on Bryan and unlocked the gate to let him eat and drink. As I watched these interactions, I came to realize that horses know so much more about community and fair play than most people think.

Mustang had a certain look in his eye that showed his intelligence. He had a way of looking into the distance, not with fear, but with awareness. Many books speak of this look, calling it the "look of eagles." When Mustang was corralled, that look grew more intense. He would stand at the fence, gazing far away to where the desert floor met the mountains. He would stare, toss his head, dance and then look again, smelling the air as he caught sight of his place of origin.

I often wondered if Mustang's early life as a wild stallion had shaped his remarkable intelligence and caretaking qualities. Although I was able to experience my horses in the desert, I knew there was more to be learned by experiencing a community of wild horses whose survival depended completely on the land and on sticking together. My adventures with my horses taught me much about community interaction, but I knew a piece was still missing. I believed I could find this piece by going to the wild and experiencing Mustang's life for myself. To run with wild horses and be accepted by a herd of wild horses would unveil the mystery of Mustang's true nature. I didn't know how this would happen, but I knew somehow, someday I would go to the wild and find out what had shaped Mustang – what had given him the "eye of an eagle" and made his spirit free.

I got to know Mustang very well before an opportunity arose to interact with and study wild horses. Before taking you into that adventure, I would like to share some stories that I picked up along the way. These tales will help you understand what I was seeking and allow me to share some important lessons that shaped my understanding and appreciation of my experiences in the wild.

Chapter V

The Kelley's Grapefruit Orchard
Mustang's First Lesson

In the summertime, I rode every single day. The days I did not ride Mustang, he was welcome to come along when I rode another horse. At first, I had to pony Mustang on the horse I was riding to keep him under control, but soon I trained him to stay glued to me like a family dog without any restraint whatsoever. All I had to do when he got too far away from me was call his name and he would come back to me. He understood that when I called he needed to come and then stay close to my side. Because of an experience with Babe and me in the grapefruit orchards, he was especially obedient to my call when I rode her.

The first time I allowed Mustang to join us at liberty, I choose a particularly hot day. I thought riding in the heat would help us all stay together. I was concerned that if the day was cool, Mustang might not stay at our side. His energy would be high and he might wander off on his own.

I picked a short ride to the Kelley's grapefruit orchard as our destination. It would not be so hot there, maybe ninety degrees. Since every other place would be hotter, he would choose to stay with us there. We could all hang out together in the shade. The horses could graze on the thick summer grasses between the rows of trees.

On our ride to the orchard, Mustang followed closely. However, when we reached the orchard, Mustang and Babe started grazing furiously and didn't stick together. I stayed on Babe's back and let her decide her direction. As Mustang lost interest in us, I helped Babe go further away to see if he would eventually join us. He didn't. He couldn't care less where we went. Next time, I would remember to carry an extra halter and lead.

I started to worry. How was I going to get him home? I didn't want to ride off and leave him. He might chase after us and get hit by a car. I was going to be stuck in the orchard all afternoon.

I leaped off Babe, feeling safe that she would not leave the orchard. I knew Mustang needed a lesson. On the days I rode another horse, I wanted to be able to take Mustang along without restraint. But at this point in our relationship, if I took him along he would wander around out of my control.

I began to relax, confident that a solution would present itself. I headed off on my own to enjoy the orchard and to find a solution. As I walked through the rows, I noticed that the trees were uniform. The branches were all heavily thorned and canopied to the ground with large waxy leaves. The leaves were so thick that you could not see the tree trunk. Upon further investigation, I found that some canopies had small openings. Within the canopy I discovered large, hollow rooms, big enough to play in and big enough, I concluded, to hide myself and one horse. This was going to be Mustang's lesson in sticking with the group.

I gathered up Babe and led her even further from Mustang. We went slowly, taking our time, so as not to arouse his suspicion. When I was sure Mustang didn't know where we were, I led Babe inside one of the canopied trees. Before long, Mustang noticed we were missing.

He started neighing and running desperately through the rows. Babe called to him occasionally. Although he could hear her, he couldn't figure out where the sound was coming from. At first Babe enjoyed hiding from him and only called when he was getting out of range. Finally, taking pity on him, Babe called out when Mustang was very close. With this new information, he immediately started looking inside the trees – I could tell by the sound of rattling branches when he stuck his head inside the canopies.

After poking around a bit, he discovered us. He was genuinely annoyed with our disappearance and extremely happy to have found us. Both horses greeted each other with beautiful nickering sounds as they arched their necks and touched noses. But Mustang had to add his disapproval in his greeting with a little snap at me and a kick in the air as he was talking to Babe. I repeated our game over and over. It took most of the afternoon for me to get the result I was looking for. Mustang had to learn that it was his job to keep an eye on us and stay close. I had no idea that I could accomplish the result I was looking for but when I had finished our hide-and-seek games, Mustang was completely under control and never again wandered away when I was riding another horse. After our time in the Kelley's grapefruit orchard, I could take him anywhere and have him stay as close as if I were ponying him. To get him to follow me when I was riding Babe, I had only to ride away from him. He would always run to catch up.

That afternoon in the grapefruit trees I became aware of the importance of working with horses in a natural setting without fences and that I could use a horse's desire for companionship as a training method. Mustang and Babe showed me that horses have a natural desire to stick together. I learned about the power of the draw and how to use it.

My focus today for training horses is designed to be fun and entertaining for the horse. I believe there is a bond that exists naturally between horses and humans. The root of this bond lies in a universal language that is shared by all living things, a universal language that creates natural teamwork. My methods of training rely on this bond, a bond of friendship first.

Using the draw has been the cornerstone of all my work with horses and forms the foundation of my Liberty Training, Beyond the Whisper™ method. It is important that my work does not get confused with the current horsemanship in round-pens. I use a round-pen only for advanced training, when a horse is already trained and bonded to me at liberty and has developed a full ability to enjoy and understand how to circle, walk, trot, canter and turn on command. Starting in a round pen without a bond in the performance creates a feeling of powerlessness. The horse loses his self-respect by not being able to trust his own instinct for getting out of a jam of emotional trauma.

Restricting a horse to a round-pen until he comes to terms with his predicament has little to do with my work. My method allows the horse freedom to escape anything he doesn't like doing. I never impose my will on a horse if the horse is not willing and happy to follow my lead. I only train a horse that accepts me and see me as part of his family. I don't start training until this connection is made. Relating to a horse in this way requires no more time than round-pen work, but time is not the issue in my mind. Friendship by choice, without resistance or capture, is the issue. This philosophy is my spiritual path and I have learned that I can put order in chaos and lead without entrapment or force from a unity that exists in every moment.

Krishnamurtis's introduction to *The First and Last Freedom* talks about communication.

"To communicate with one another, even if we know each other very well, is extremely difficult .... Instantaneous understanding comes when we meet on the same level at the same time."

And I would add, "… in agreement."

This sort of communication does not occur when starting a horse in a round-pen. For a horse to form a bond with a trainer in the round-pen, he must give up his rights, freedom and dignity. The trainer who uses a round-pen to establish a bond will never understand the true communication horses share with each other.

My friendship with horses came from a spontaneous language that arose from the moment. The desert was a safe experimental ground for me to learn relationships with horses without the need for fences. Because of this freedom, I learned the ways of horses that could never have been discovered without the freedom my horses and I shared together.

Chapter VI
Eggs Rancheros and the Big Race
Bareback Horsemanship

My mother cooked complete and delicious meals: a fresh salad, two vegetables and one meat item. Dessert came from the freezer or cookie jar. Occasionally we would get a casserole of macaroni and cheese or scalloped potatoes.

My mother is a great cook – she came by it naturally. It runs in her family. My father's side of the family, on the other hand, shouldn't be allowed in the kitchen. My grandmother on my father's side used the refrigerator for storing small carcasses she dissected to keep them fresh for research. Reaching into her refrigerator for that bowl of Jell-O, I more than once found myself gasping at some unfortunate frog laid open with precisely placed pins, right next to my snack. For some reason, the green Jell-O with canned pineapples and marshmallows cut into bite-sized pieces lost its charm. The fact that the uncovered bowl of green Jell-O was green didn't help. I had the feeling it was diseased from sharing the same air space with her science specimens.

Actually, I never took anything out of her refrigerator. I knew she was a bad cook. My grandmother was thin and ate strange things. She saved all her chicken bones and would make a meal out of them by slicing them open with her botany tools. She would split a bone lengthwise and shovel out the marrow, saying it was the best part of the chicken. This was often her whole meal. No bread or vegetables, no salad, nothing else – just chicken marrow cold out of the refrigerator, looking very much like the poor dead frog, only larger. I never ate anything she offered me if it was stored in the icy death trap she called a refrigerator.

My mother, on the other hand, never really used a refrigerator to store leftovers. My dad and I ate everything she prepared. The refrigerator was a place to keep staples like fresh fruit, vegetables, butter, cheese, eggs, milk, jam and pink champagne. My family had pink champagne on Sunday for breakfast with eggs rancheros.

While my mother prepared breakfast, I helped in the kitchen cleaning vegetables, scrubbing celery and removing the strings, and chopping the onions. We were careful to make enough for the drop-in guests that often came.

Many Sundays, when it would come time to peel and chop the onions, there were none to be found. My mother would have to drive to the market and sometimes there was no time for that. We couldn't ask my father. My father would be cleaning the pool or washing the cars or working on a broken-down tractor – whatever he was doing, it was a bad idea to interrupt his work. My dad worked as if he hated what he was doing. If you interrupted him, he would turn on you like a mad badger, spewing cuss words, kicking what he was working on, and saying in a very loud voice, "What do you want?" – which meant, if you told him, you'd be sorry. I never told my father what I wanted. It just brought on a whole bunch of unnecessary trouble.

My family loved onions and missed them if they were left out. This is the way it was with my mother's eggs rancheros. In fact, my father wouldn't touch the eggs rancheros without onions and would hold my mother responsible for an inedible breakfast.

I can't remember exactly when the idea of a pony express delivery service dawned on me, but it was a great idea. I could get out of kitchen work and at the same time ride my horse. And Babe could do what she liked best but seldom had the chance to do – run! I was looking to break the sound barrier, to relive the pony express, to give Babe her exercise, to save the day, and to eat eggs rancheros with onions. Town was a mile and a half away. I could race to town, bring back the onions, and be a hero.

The plan worked. We never had to do without onions again, thanks to Babe. With fifty cents in my pocket for two onions, I would run down to the barn, jump on Babe bareback and race at top speed into town. Babe would run whether or not she was asked. She always wanted to run. She came from a rent string where she spent her whole life running before she came to us at 12 years of age. She was like those people who go through life so quickly they have no time for anything but speed.

Riding Babe was like riding a sawhorse. Her style of prancing was a pulverizing experience that could have cracked walnuts between me and the saddle.

When I got to the market, I had to move fast. I would pull Babe up short, rein her back in the opposite direction to slow her down, and jump off at the same time, just like a pony express rider. I would tie her up, run into the store, grab the onions, be polite, and find a way back on, which was a challenge. Ever eager to run, she reared her objection while I held her back long enough to leap onto her from a fence or a rock – or a car bumper, if no one was looking.

Many times a passing car would slow down and travel along with us for a while, reporting to me out the window how fast we were going. I would urge Babe on a little faster, whispering loudly in her ear, "Babe, go-go! Babe, go-go-go-go-go!" Then she would really try, as someone in the car next to us would report, "Thirty-three, now thirty-four, now thirty-five! You are going thirty-six miles an hour!"

Babe really came alive when she felt like she could beat a car. Even the people in the car could feel her enthusiasm. A couple of times they even let us win, so Babe could feel good about herself. She seemed to change after that. Her gait became more pleasant and she started to show more personality around the barn.

With a year's worth of running into town for onions and after learning that we were running about the same speed as racehorses (though some people argued that a car speedometer was not as good a measure as a stop watch) I knew that we were surprisingly fast. Some people thought we would run even faster on a racetrack. I never knew for sure if their reports of how fast we were going weren't a little exaggerated.

Behind our ranch, about a mile away, was a breeding ranch for racehorses. Cecil's father owned the ranch, and I rode with Cecil occasionally. I was eleven and Cecil was twelve.

One day I talked Cecil into a race, pitting one of his dad's race-horses against Babe. Cecil and I negotiated the details. I wanted to race two miles. Cecil wanted to race one mile. I wanted the race as long as possible because I knew the racehorse would run out of steam. Cecil knew it, too. We quibbled for a few days and finally settled on a quarter of a mile. I knew his racehorse could barely reach top speed in such a short distance.

One afternoon, Cecil showed me the horse I would be racing against. The horse was a beautiful Appaloosa racehorse, and Cecil let me ride him. Like Babe, he loved to run, and because racehorses are large animals, it felt like I was riding a building. He was the largest horse I had ever ridden (Babe was only about 14.2 hands.). I rode him bareback and he had that same sawhorse feel as Babe. My heart was in my throat at being on this strange, super-powered racehorse, but I loved it. For a child, there is nothing like being able to keep a strong, high-spirited horse under control and acting nonchalant about it.

Cecil thought the race was laughable and wanted to scare me by putting me on his dad's horse. It was his way of rubbing my nose into the reality of my challenge. He teased me all afternoon about how bad he was going to beat us. He delighted over my silly idea that an aged mustang like Babe could even begin to keep up with his racehorse. He said that he had respected my ability with horses, but he knew now that he had been mistaken. Having said that, while sitting on his dad's horse, he spat into a bush as an act of disgust. I made no comment. Bragging before the race seemed backward to me. I would save my comments for later. If Cecil lost, I knew I would have to listen to a barrage of excuses. Being around Cecil was always an uncomfortable experience.

I picked the location of the race – a grape vineyard on our ranch. We would run through the rows of grapes. I knew better than to trust Cecil. He hated girls and most definitely would cheat if he had the chance. The grape rows would keep him from crowding into Babe and me.

I often rode with a group of boys, my closest neighbors. There was Ralph Paulee, (his dad was our family doctor,) Cecil and Cecil's younger brother. Cecil was always out for a practical joke, and I had to be on the alert for the consequences of riding with him. However, everything he tried was in vain because I was far more capable of handling his pranks than he figured.

I remember once while riding Mustang, Cecil slid by and pulled Mustang's bridle off. Can you imagine that? Then he hit Mustang on the rump to make him run away with me. His trick didn't work because I usually rode Mustang without a bridle and only used one when we were around other horses! So when Cecil pulled his little stunt, I tied Mustang's bridle to my saddle and informed Cecil that

I had trained my horse to ride without one – and what did he think of that!

The sparse desert population created odd companions. Ralph was polite and nice as could be and loved his horse like I loved mine. Cecil's brother tried to emulate all three of us; he was the youngest and wanted to be liked by all. Cecil was hard to figure. The dynamics between us were strange – but still we rode together.

I never had much to say when I rode with friends. My mind was occupied with the nuances and subtleties that Mustang and I were discovering together. The desert, the creatures we might find there and the unpredictability of what lay ahead provided the adventure. Riding with others was an interruption. When I rode with the boys, I was surprised to find that I enjoyed riding alone more.

On the day of the race, we were all four there. I personally didn't have a clue who would win the race. Cecil and I both rode bareback to reduce our horse's load as well as to show our prowess as skilled riders.

Even though Ralph was on my side, he told me that I was probably going to lose. However, he told Cecil there was no way his horse could beat me because he had seen Babe run.

I knew Cecil would try to jump the gate before Ralph yelled, "Go!" My strategy was to let him go ahead and cheat. If we started even, he would complain that I jumped the gate whether I had or not. As it was, he still complained that I jumped the gate and we had three false starts. Cecil wasn't happy unless he was cheating.

By the time I had pulled up Babe three times, she had worked herself into a frenzy. She realized what I was going to ask of her. I could feel her say to Cecil's horse, "Watch out, big boy, you are only one horse. I beat 300 horses [horsepower] last week and I am faster than those speedy automobiles."

Ralph yelled one last time, "Go!"

Cecil indeed jumped the gate and took the lead. His horse maintained the lead halfway through the rows. At the halfway mark, Babe started gaining on the racehorse like a locomotive. She increased her speed at every stride. I had no part in the race except to stay with her and not be a burden. There was no need for me even to say, "Go Babe!" once we left the line.

Cecil won by a nose, but on the very next stride, Babe took the lead.

We were all happy. Babe thought she won. Cecil knew he won, though he was visibly shaken. He didn't even brag after the race. He just said something about winning and slipped quietly away back to his ranch. I knew Babe was, in fact, a phenomenal, once-in-a-lifetime runner. I couldn't help wondering how the race would have turned out had she been a three-year old. However, Babe felt she was at the top of her career; after all, in her mind she was beating racehorses and automobiles.

After the race, I went home to help with dinner; my job was to set the table and make the salad. When I told my family about what Babe had accomplished, Dad said he had to agree with me that we did own quite a gal. I was proud of her and happy to give her another day to shine. It was a great adventure, but I had no desire to enter Babe in competitive racing. Running for onions for our eggs rancheros was my only interest, apart from getting out of the kitchen.

After dinner and washing the dishes, I called my grandmother to tell her the news. She invited me over for Jell-O and cookies. As I was putting the butter back into our refrigerator, it occurred to me that it would be a good idea to put a couple large napkins in the pockets of my overalls. I might need a way to ditch Grandma's Jell-O; I surely wouldn't be eating it!

Chapter VII

Destined to Meet
I Discover My Magnetism

It is odd how adventure sometimes shows up when you least expect it. What was about to take place was a turning point in my life. I wound up with my first job, but more than that, I discovered my magnetism.

One summer day, when the sun had driven everyone else into the shade, I started out on Mustang, riding across the desert. I rode with just a loose rope around his neck – no bit or metal, cinch, saddle or halter, nothing that would burn him or overheat his body. We were out looking for magical oases, man-made or otherwise. I had soaked Mustang and myself with well water I had pumped into the cistern minutes earlier. It felt like liquid ice and raised goose bumps the size of small volcanoes. The slight, burning breeze was now bearable, but I knew it wouldn't be for long. We would dry in less than an hour.

We started out with thoughts of cool places where we could rest and then ride on. We rode along in the shadows of tamarisk trees and rested beneath mesquite bushes that formed tunnels and large, secret, unseen rooms. We found standpipes bursting with water, irrigating row crops; these were perfect for Mustang to drink from and for soaking our hot bodies. We kept searching for a magical land that we could share together – and found it in a date palm grove under irrigation.

Date groves were the sole human contribution to the desert that seemed appropriate and beneficial because of the shade they offered. Date groves were formed with dikes that held up to a foot and a half of water. The dikes were built in large quadrants around the date palms, creating the most glorious oasis-like conditions.

When the water dried up, it left grasslands that were shaded by the umbrellas of tall date palms that reached at least twenty feet in the air, high enough to allow the desert breeze to cool us from the sun. It was a hide-a-way and picnic ground I took advantage of frequently. Just Mustang and me, alone, like Lawrence of Arabia.

When we reached our favorite date grove, we found they were indeed irrigating. It was an oasis of cool water, tall grass and shade. Our entry routine was always the best part. In fact, it was pure joy. Mustang took off running and leaped over the dike, cantering through water splashing well above our heads like a fountain. The mud was thick and deep and each progressive step slowly brought Mustang to his knees. He collapsed and fell to its beckoning invitation. Before trying to get up, he lay in the water, pulling and eating the grasses growing out of the water. With me still on, he climbed to his feet once again to paw and splash. Every movement he made resonated through my body. Then he dropped his head, his nose brushing briskly back and forth, throwing water everywhere, sweeping away the floating matter so he could take a clean, cool drink of fresh water. We had found our paradise.

Already wet from the splashing fountain Mustang's entry had created, I jumped into the soggy mire with him. I ran leaping and splashing water into the air, falling, sitting, lying and rolling in the water, laughing and screaming. I submerged, holding my breath. I felt I could stay under as long as an alligator in a Florida swamp. When I ran out of air, I sprang up out of the water and then dove under again, holding my breath and lying quiet as an alligator taking a nap. After thoroughly exhausting myself, I lay floating in the mud and muck, looking up through the trees, watching the dragonflies zig-zagging above my head and counting the other flying insects our splashing water had attracted.

Finally, I sat waist deep in the water, resting my back against a dike with dripping, wet hair tangled in date palm debris, grass clippings and a few, unfortunate insects. I was wet, muddy and quite pleased with my dishevelment. I sat in a stupor looking into the desert, not blinking, at one with the moment and our beautiful surroundings. These moments when we hung out together were the best part of our relationship. I noticed how happily Mustang gazed at the water's surface among the floating debris that shifted around, making way for our presence. As my mind started classifying everything in the water and possibly in my hair, something stirred on the horizon.

Mustang jerked his head up while every muscle in his body hardened. I stared into the heat waves at a speck in the distance that was growing at an alarming rate. I could tell that whatever it was, it was traveling very fast. A strange sound accompanied it. My heart raced. The desert very seldom produced anything other than mirages in late July, but this mirage was coming fast and started taking the shape of a camel heading directly for me at top speed.

It was not a mirage; it was most definitely a miracle. There were no camels in this desert, but there he was, very unhappy and coming directly to me. He appeared to come on wings. A camel, wearing a halter and lead. He came to me . . . for what? What was my mother going to say when I told her he followed me home? Watching his demeanor, I made a decision. He came to me for protection. My reaction was as quick as his approach. To Mustang's surprise and before the camel had time to respond, I threw my arms around him.

Without hesitation, before I had time to consider what I was doing, I found myself in an out-of-control intimacy and affection for my newfound, distressed friend. I was drawn to him beyond my control. Every part of him looked touchable. His hair was woolly soft and hung from his body in light puffs of golden locks. As I reached deep into his coat to feel his body, he felt like he was made up of stuck-together down pillows. I rubbed and scratched him deeply to soothe his frayed nerves. As he began to relax, I gazed into his eyes and looked at his head carefully. I had never been this close to a camel before. I wiggled his jaw and lifting his top lip, I found his lips separated in the middle. It was, I could tell, his natural condition. As I continued my inspection, I realized that a camel is a strange beast and a joy to behold.

I cupped his eyes in my hands and felt them roll around under his poochy lids like butterfly wings and fuzzy caterpillars. I examined his long eyelashes, poked his nose and wobbled his lips. He settled down and stayed very close to me, always blocking my path and keeping face to face. I took his lead cautiously and asked him gently to obey a slight tug on the line. He gave in easily. I tried leading him around and asking him to halt. He was very happy to comply and seemed to feel more comfortable and secure putting himself in my charge. I started making stronger and stronger leading and halting requests to check his tolerance. He definitely wanted to obey me. It was obvious he had chosen me. I asked myself no more questions about his plausibility; it was set, he was mine.

I was holding the lead rope and the camel had relaxed and was grazing when four men came running up, screaming and waving their arms.

"Let go of the rope! Back away! He's dangerous!" they yelled. "He just broke a man's arm!"

By now I looked presentable. My hair had dried and there was no mess left on me from my playing in the water; the desert almost always brushes right off. I didn't want to scream. I wanted to talk in a civilized manner. I had been taught to respect my elders and never to raise my voice, but I had no choice. Screaming was the only way they could hear me – they were afraid to come close enough to be heard without shouting.

I screamed, "He is not dangerous! He likes me."

To demonstrate, I led him around and petted him. Not impressed, they were still afraid for my safety and nervously approached. When they got twenty feet or so from me, the camel lunged at them. As I pulled him back, he started bawling, his mouth wide open, expressing extreme rage and contempt for these men. I appreciated how he still had the presence of mind not to turn on me. I could not understand why he had chosen me as his savior, but he very obviously had, so I stood my ground. I told them that he was my camel and that I was going to take him home with me.

I was feeling very protective. Obviously these men must have abused him in some way. I had already figured out how I could properly house and care for him. The camel was making my decision easy by continuing his threats toward the men's advances. We all stood our ground, arguing and gesturing and yelling, with added remarks from the camel who had now taken to spitting along with bawling.

Mustang stayed cool and showed no interest in our dispute. If I needed his help, he would have stepped in the middle of the dispute and put an end to it. Mustang didn't like men and would never let a man get close to me or to him, but these guys were keeping their distance. Mustang could see the camel was taking care of that.

I really had no choice in the matter. Eventually the men made me understand that I was going to have to return the camel no matter how we had bonded to each other, but the camel did not agree with our decision and refused to accept the transfer. He had escaped from the fairgrounds about a quarter of a mile away, so I consented to lead him back for them. I explained the plan to Mustang and warned the men to keep their distance from me, not just for the camel's sake, but because of the greater possibility that my horse would also attack them. Mustang was a bigger threat because he was loose, and I couldn't lead the camel and Mustang at the same time. The men were building up a healthy respect for my abilities, because of how the camel was behaving toward me and how Mustang seemed to understand and take direction from me but always with a flat ear held tight toward them.

I learned that the fairgrounds had purchased camels as an added theme attraction for our date festival. They planned to ride the camels in costume in the parade and use them in a nightly pageant and on the weekends for camel races. Unfortunately, the people in charge weren't camel oriented, or if they were, they didn't impress me much.

We all paraded back to the fairgrounds without a word. None of us were sure how the camel would react to his return trip. We picked up an audience on our way back to the fairgrounds. We explained the precarious situation to every new person we encountered and asked them to follow at a distance. It ended up a sizable parade, but quiet as a funeral. We were all on alert, with no one trusting the circumstances or each other. I am sure all of us had our own private thoughts. My concern was about turning the camel over to these men, even if I had already given my consent.

When we got to the camel's home, I was surprised to find it was a real camel tent containing five other camels and two babies. It amazed me how organized the camel tent was. They had neat, well-made beds of straw and each camel had a small place designated by straw bales. Some camels had large places and others had just enough room to lie down. My new friend took to his bed and seemed pleased to be back. I spent the rest of the day hanging out with him. The men told me their personal stories, sharing what they did know about camels. Mustang stayed around the tent and grazed in the date grove surrounding the fairgrounds.

After plenty of talk, the men decided it would be a good thing for me to come back the next day in case they had trouble with the camel. They offered me the high position of camel groom. If I did a good job each day, my pay would be that I would get to come back and work again the next day. We struck a deal!

It turned out to be a great job. I got to hold the camel before the parades, the pageant, the camel races and interviews. It was my first non-paying, outside job with benefits. Because the camel was kept inside the fairgrounds, I got an entrance pass I could use any time I wanted – which was every day – and the pass was good for several years thereafter.

This camel encounter held a very important message for me. Before he found me, I suspected I had a special gift with animals, but I wasn't totally convinced. After this episode with the camel, I knew that I had an instant rapport with animals that was undeniable. I had discovered my magnetism.

This adventure is part of a tapestry woven from my everyday experiences riding Mustang in the hot Coachella Valley and from a rare day when a camel came to me across the desert. He came because he heard our joyfulness and he needed an oasis he could call "home."

Chapter VIII

Tashay, the Magnetic Fool
The Power of Positive Thinking

I need to diverge momentarily from the path of my childhood to recount my most notable lesson in magnetism. The camel opened my eyes to my own personal power, to believe in my magnetism without question. The 'without question' was the most important part. Beliefs based upon little need all the support they can get.

The most amazing use of magnetism I have ever experienced came from a complete stranger. He opened my eyes to practical application of magnetism and the importance of a personal confidence that I could accomplish anything – even if I'd never experienced it before. This underlying confidence is absolutely essential in becoming a tactful horse trainer.

I was in my twenties living in Carmel Highlands, California at the time that I met Tashay. Walking through a forest near my home, I ran across a funny sight. A young man was desperately trying to put a halter on a young horse. He was in a fairly large corral with four matched bay Standardbreds. Managing to hold one of them between himself and a tree, he was trying to force an upside down halter onto its head. He was doing a fairly good job of it, at that, even though it was never truly going to fit. By the manner of their behavior, I could tell that all four horses were untrained, and I wondered what he planned to do with them. Surely, he was no horseman. I half suspected he was trying to steal someone else's horses. I knew I needed to find out what was going on.

As I approached him I became aware that he was extremely handsome. I was attracted to his good looks and did my best not to let it show. He was tall and thin with a perfect muscular build. He had longish, blond hair. He was wearing tall military boots that buckled at the top, but because they were not buckled, they jingled in his struggle with the horse. It was the sound of his boots that first caught my attention. I asked what he was planning to do with the horse he was holding. He told me that he had just been hired to break and train these horses into a hitch of four to haul tourists in carriages through the streets of Carmel. When I asked him what experience and qualifications he had for such a job, he told me, "None." I asked him how he planned to accomplish the task. He explained that he had four horses, a carriage, harnesses and a book on how to break and train a team of four horses. I asked if he knew how to drive a team and he said he had never driven even a single horse.

I offered to help him with the halter and he introduced himself as Tashay. He was glad to see me and glad for the help. I told him that the job he was undertaking was not practical and that should he succeed, he would probably be the first to ever accomplish such a feat. He laughed and said he had been given the required amount of time the book suggested and he planned to accomplish his task over the next six months. He asked me to explain the harness, so we laid it out on the ground and I did my best. I told him of my abilities for breaking single hitches. He seemed pleased, but oddly, not surprised. It was as though he somehow knew someone would come along with the skills he needed for this impossible task.

That afternoon, I gave him all the advice I could muster. He pointed out that it was a fairly simple task, especially now that he had more information from me. I offered my help over the next six months, though I told him that I was not qualified to make a team of four two-year olds street-safe for a carriage service. He said not to worry; that was his job.

I was relieved, which caused me to relax and give it my best effort. Imagine that; I was relieved that a total fool was in charge of a project that I, as a professional horse trainer, was not capable of accomplishing. Somehow I had taken on a task I didn't believe in and all without pay, and I was calling him the fool.

In reality, the project had many perks. I wanted to learn how to train a team of horses and this would be a great opportunity. It was an odd situation but somehow I felt whatever the outcome, it was going to prove to be a valuable horse training lesson. Seldom is one asked to be part of a project like this, a project that starts with horses only partially halter broken and ends with a steadfast team of four. There were many holes in my knowledge of horse training and here was an opportunity to advance my education.

I told Tashay that we needed more than a book, carriage, harnesses and me. What we truly needed was a seasoned professional in training carriage horses. I explained that even after the horses were trained, it would take years to season them. Only then would they be truly dependable and considered safe to drive as a public service.

Again Tashay told me that he would take one step at a time. He was sure that someone with the skills to finish the job would show up to help us. In the meantime, we could get the horses well on their way. If no one showed up, it meant that we could get the job done ourselves.

During the weeks that followed, Tashay and I worked on gentling the horses and teaching them manners. Weeks turned into months. The people who hired Tashay were not concerned about the time it was taking; that was a true blessing.

For six months, Tashay and I were with each other most of the time. Either we were training the horses, running errands or just having fun. We became inseparable.

When we first started working together, Tashay didn't have a plan and neither did I. But at least I knew where to begin. The first step was to evaluate what the horses knew. Well, that was easy as they had hardly any training. The training that they had received only taught them that they did not want to be trained. I felt that this attitude was the first issue we needed to address. It made sense to Tashay that this should be our primary focus.

We spent the first day with them in their corral. They became comfortable with our presence. The next day we did the same thing, only we fed them carrots in the afternoon. In three days they had the routine down. Once they understood the routine, we could easily put halters on them while they were eating the carrots. On the fifth day we put their halters on before giving them carrots. In a week's time, Sport, Tony, Lad and Dandy were thinking that training was a good thing.

When we started, they would run away from us if we had halters in our hands. In our first week, they were already letting us tie them to a tree for a few hours. Carriage horses often stand still for long periods of time between rides. In the beginning, Tashay tied them at a time that they normally took their naps. After their naps, there were always more carrots to eat.

The next phase of their training was a lot of fun. It is most important to prepare a horse to have the right attitude about learning new things. The horse needs to like being with the people who are training them. The most important thing to develop in a horse is his trust; he needs to know that his trainer is going to take care of him and protect him from danger. Sport, Tony, Lad and Dandy were now ready to trust us enough to be led off the property and do some exploring.

I knew that the next step in their education should be getting used to traffic. This would prepare them for traveling as a team pulling a carriage though the streets of Carmel. A seasoned team of horses that knew only quiet country driving would probably be scared to death working on public streets. A scared team is like a lit match next to a stick of dynamite. In seconds, a scared team can become a dangerous time bomb. As green as these horses would be, I knew that getting them used to new places, traffic, surprise encounters, strangers, cars and barking dogs was most important.

We accomplished this by walking them in hand through the neighborhood where they were housed. Tashay and I each took one horse. We left the other two horses in their corral or tied. We walked the horses all over the Carmel Highlands, up and down its residential streets. We had a great time, laughing and talking with the neighbors on our way each day.

Carmel Highlands is one of the most beautiful places in the world. The highland homes are a collection of charming cottages tucked in nooks of nature, one more enchanting than the next. Pines, ferns and fauna similar to the natural botanicals found in the Scottish highlands frame the many ocean views. The people living in the highlands are often a bit reclusive. Famous writers and artists such as Ansel Adams, Kim Novak and Joan Baez lived there at the time. Ordinarily, it would be very hard to meet the residents, but we got to know many of our neighbors who enjoyed the horses and developed an interest in their progress.

The horses got used to the streets and moving cars. Cars passed only occasionally, but when they did, it was a total surprise as they sped around bends at breakneck speeds. We had to walk the horses beside the road on a path no wider than a narrow walking path.

Many times, neighbors would stop their cars to talk and once or twice someone gave carrots to the horses. Soon the horses understood that within every car was a possible treat. It turned out to be the perfect place to prepare the horses for working the streets of Carmel. There was plenty of uphill and downhill, zigging and zagging down country lanes. Barking dogs, walkers, bikers, cars and even deer could meet us around a bend in the road when we least expected it. A sudden surprise in a totally serene atmosphere was the perfect venue to season the horses.

When the horses were quite used to the routine and willing to walk ahead of us on the trail, Tashay and I began walking all four horses together, single file down the winding roads. I took two horses, one in front of me and one behind me, and Tashay did the same. Soon, we were able to ground drive a single hitch. Tashay would drive one horse and I would drive another. The other two stayed tied at home.

We trained for just a couple of hours each day. The rest of the day we spent together. Many times Tashay and I hitchhiked down to Nepenthe's in Big Sur State Park. Tashay always talked about philosophy and the great minds of history. He was no ivory tower philosopher; he used philosophy to help him make things work. That is why he took the job training the horses. He told me that he felt that he could do anything he wanted to accomplish because he knew how to get help from the universe that surrounded him. He said that the universe is always there to support us if we stay positive, focused and willing to do the work that it takes to accomplish our goals.

At night we would go to the library and Tashay would pick out books for me to read on metaphysics. Carmel had a lot of books on metaphysics. In the sixties, everyone our age was interested in the magic of life and finding good vibrations.

Many times we would hitchhike to the Thunderbird Bookstore and Café in Carmel Valley. All the local people gathered here to sit around, talk and peruse the books. The food was great and the owner did not care how many books we looked through during the course of our lunch. Lunch often took up most of the afternoon.

On one of our visits to the bookstore, we met Jim. Jim was the next piece of the puzzle. We found him right when we needed him, just as Tashay had said it would happen. I felt that the horses were as far along in their training as Tashay and I could take them.

Jim was a tall, heavyset man in his early 40's. He had broken and trained many teams of horses. I could not believe our good fortune. When Jim showed up, Tashay enjoyed pointing out to me how the universe provides. He reminded me of Don Quixote; I was his Sancho Panza.

After meeting the horses, Jim was interested and took over our project. He agreed with me that they were ready to be driven together as a team. Jim helped us with every step and taught Tashay how to drive a four up. In fact, Jim was hired to work under Tashay. That was amazing because most owners, upon finding a person of Jim's experience, would have fired Tashay, but they didn't. This was another miracle Tashay was able pull out of the hat.

Jim would not have wanted to be involved in the initial training of the horses, but because we had them driving so well, he was willing to help. Jim got to do the part of the training that he enjoyed, putting the horses together as a team. I got to watch and learn.

He first hitched one of the green horses alongside a seasoned driving horse. The green horse quickly learned his job from the seasoned horse. This formula in Jim's expert hand made the process seem almost mundane.

Eventually the horses were moved to the valley to be closer to Jim. Even though I wasn't present for a lot of the actual breaking and training of a team, I still learned a lot. At least I have a good idea of how the process works.

Tashay felt that he could have accomplished the feat without help from Jim or me. Whether that was true or not wasn't relevant because Tashay always found the help he needed.

Tashay accomplished his goal, and this accomplishment was even more phenomenal than I had originally suspected. He asked me to go with him on his first day driving the team in Carmel. In confidence – because he didn't want anyone else to know – he told me that he had poor eyesight and needed me to point out the stop signs because he couldn't see them. A couple of spins around the route were enough for him to learn where the stop signs were.

Tashay and I remained friends for many years. He was charming and could put harmony and natural order in things he didn't understand. He saw the purpose in everything. He was a philosopher, a nature lover and a man who knew no strangers. He told me he looked for the good in everything, and he spoke of the importance of perception by choice. He felt that choosing the right perception would lead to accomplishing his goals. He believed in his magnetism and that it had attracted me to him! I guess I was Tashay's camel. I learned from Tashay that first you must stand-alone, then you must be willing to be guided by others, and then magnetic energy will support your dreams, impossible as they might seem.

Together we were magnetic fools. He was my teacher in believing in the power of believing, and I was his unqualified advisor with a green four-up in a time when things worked. I learned from him that if you want something, go start it and help will arrive. He was a genius in fool's clothing. I impacted a moment in his life, and he impacted a lifetime in mine.

Chapter IX

Leaping Lizards, Watch Widows and Scorpion Tales

Three Stages of Coexistence

Returning to my childhood experiences on the ranch when I was 8, my chores began at 6:30 am; so did my horsemanship. Over time I came to look for, and find, horsemanship principles even in my everyday chores.

My daily chores included cleaning the water troughs, folding the baling wire, raking loose hay, weeding, filling the cistern, sweeping the pump room floor and ridding it of cobwebs. From the time I started until the time I finished, my morning chores were interrupted by all sorts of surprising encounters.

Like most 8 year olds, I would have preferred to sleep in. I mustered up my energy as I got dressed. Once out the door, I became a horse, making my way down the road prancing, running, bucking and leaping to the barn site four hundred yards behind our house.

Every morning on my journey to the horse barn, I was ambushed by two large lizards. I tried to run by them as quickly as possible, thinking that if I hurried, they would leave me alone. They never did. They leaped out at me – and always from the same spot, about halfway between the house and the barn. Over time, my fear of them increased from the sheer predictability of their ambush.

They were the size of ground squirrels, but with longer bodies. Their bodies were pure white with chocolate brown freckles. The freckles along their sides were the size of raindrops, increasing to the size of dimes over the tops of their backs. Their tails were even longer than their bodies.

The two of them would jump out as I passed, standing up on their hind legs like something out of the horror movie *The Day the Lizards Ran!* In an upright position, they were easily nineteen inches tall. They would charge me in unison, their legs whirling like eggbeaters. My dad told me that they were harmless – but when I charged them back, they were unimpressed. Even though my attack stopped them from charging at me, it didn't stop them from standing even taller and waiting for me with gaping mouths as if they wanted to swallow me whole.

As time went on, they got braver, making longer runs and adding more terrifying displays. I dreaded their morning charge. Even today, I have a phobia about white lizards. They truly frightened me – and they seemed to enjoy it. If I hadn't shown up as expected, I believe they would have come knocking at our door, looking for me. I was less afraid of coming upon rattlesnakes in the hay than I was of meeting those two reptiles.

I have to thank them, though, for improving my skills with horses. The lizards taught me two valuable lessons: First, how a small, harmless animal can frighten a much larger animal, and second, how body language can be used for self-protection and to gain respect. These fundamental lessons in body language paved the way to communicating with horses. At the time, I did not appreciate the lesson. My sole desire was to get away from the lizards as fast as I could.

After escaping the lizards and finishing my other chores, I would head for the pump house. There my job was to clear away the cobwebs to make a path to the pump switch and check the saddle pads and saddles for black widows. These industrious little creatures built new webs every night, so this chore was never ending.

In the desert, all pump houses are crawling with black widow spiders. Fortunately, black widows hide in the day. Unfortunately, they hide in their surroundings – in this case, in the horses' tack. Whenever I entered the pump house, my skin would spring to full alert. It could detect anything that touched me, from an alfalfa leaf to an unexpected shift of clothing. It was a very awakening experience.

Despite the very real threat of a black widow's bite, I liked the fact that the pump house was safe by day but a dangerous place after dark. Black widows are non-aggressive and run and hide when someone approaches. At night, however, they are all out on their webs and accidentally walking through a web could lead to a bite. Their bite can be deadly. There is no mistaking a black widow's web; it is far stronger than other spider webs. They create a random crisscross pattern. I had heard that they are not instant biters and that if one got on me, there would be time to brush it off. I don't know if that is true, but it did make me less afraid.

Most ranchers learn to live with their problems and seek some sort of harmony before they feel a need for eradication; that was the way it was with our black widow problem. In all the years that people entered that pump house and used my tack, no one ever got bitten or even had to brush a spider from their clothes.

Like the lizards, the black widows were great teachers. They taught me to look for the underlying good in things that on the surface seem bad. Their lesson was one of peaceful coexistence, the kind that lives and lets live. Coexisting safely with other creatures – even dangerous creatures – is achieved by learning the creature's habits and behavior. It was this understanding that allowed me to find the balance point between intimacy and distance in my inter-actions with wild horses.

The pump house is now over fifty years old, still in operation and still a sanctuary for black widows. It is amazing to think that of the ones that live there today, I knew their great-great-great-great-great-great-great-great . . . grandparents, of which I never killed a single, solitary one. There simply wasn't a need to kill one once I understood the formula for coexisting. It is obvious that their ecology was working and has been working these past fifty or sixty years. They have thrived and survived without increasing in num-ber. They never became epidemic or tried to take up residence in our home, nor would they have been welcome.

Scorpions were just as unwelcome in our home, but not as polite. They invited themselves into the house about every six months. I didn't like scorpions at all; in fact, I could never figure out why God created such a creature. At least black widows were useful. They performed a service in exchange for their room and board. We kept our expensive tack in the unlocked pump house, a fact known to many people. With the black widows around, there was no need to lock. We didn't have a watchdog, a fence, an alarm system, patrol, warning signs, or any house light on for protection because we had Watch Widows on guard; we had no concern for the safety of our tack.

Scorpions were another story. They were more of a threat and could be found almost anywhere. One day, I found one in my bed. I had overslept. My mother came to wake me up and get me going on my chores. Instead of getting up, I rolled over – onto a scorpion. Instantly, I received a painful, burning sting.

I leaped out of bed and pulled back the sheets. There he was, tail up and very angry. I carefully identified him, because some scorpion stings can be fatal. This one didn't look like the dangerous kind, but I wasn't an expert. I then looked to see if I had hurt him and got a little worried. His tail was bent, like a tow truck with a bent hoist. I couldn't think of anything worse than to have to put him out of his misery. I could already hear the crunch he would make. I ran and got a fishbowl and scooped him up to show my mother and the doctor what had stung me.

By this time, the site of the sting was swollen and hurting badly. It had turned black and raised up about an inch. The swelling was about four inches across. I was sure it was serious. So was my mother. She raced me to the doctor, though I walked slowly so as not to push the poison through my bloodstream. I had heard that this is how one should walk if bitten by a rattlesnake.

We took the scorpion in the fishbowl to show the doctor. The doctor looked at my leg and looked at the scorpion. He said that the sting was absolutely harmless and that there was nothing he could give me that would make it any better. He said that the pain would eventually go away. I wondered if he would have been as nonchalant if the scorpion had stung him. Anyway, I was glad to learn I was going to live, but I kept a close eye on my leg and my symptoms. After all, with his attitude, the doctor could be wrong and it was my life at stake.

Since the doctor gave me hope about my recovery, I relaxed and considered what I should do with the scorpion now inhabiting my fishbowl. First, I named him "Tom." I decided to see if I could make a pet out of him. It was going to be difficult, because I hated scorpions. I could hardly look at one. They gave me the creeps. I didn't like spiders, bugs, or snakes. Even so, I really couldn't miss this opportunity of having another pet, no matter how repugnant. For some reason, I felt I had to find a way to break down the barriers between us. I needed a better attitude about scorpions. I knew I had to forgive him for stinging me, and he had to forgive me for rolling onto him and capturing him against his will. He wasn't very healthy after our collision, so I didn't feel wrong about keeping him imprisoned. In his condition, he might die if I didn't tend to his needs and protect him from predators.

After a week of protection, warmth and hand feeding, Tom seemed better. His tail looked almost upright. I placed him in our kitchen window on the north side of the house, overlooking our swimming pool.

After a while, I realized I could tell what my scorpion was looking at by his body language. Tom could distinguish me from other people, possibly by differences in body language or electrical vibrations, or by the interchanging patterns of set movements that identified our relationship. I fed him flies. We came to trust each other enough for him to take a fly from my hand without trying to sting me. I think he could tell that the different parts of my body were all part of a whole. Every time he would take a fly he would cock his head up and look into my eyes.

Everyone in my family enjoyed watching him in his fishbowl. In the mornings, Tom would entertain us by playing in the sand like a little child. I could even get him to dance for company. I would dial in music on the radio. If I lifted my arms to the music, he would lift his pincers. If I stepped back, he would step forward; if I stepped forward, he would step back. If I wiggled, he would, too. Friends and relatives would drop in to see him dance, and he became quite an attraction.

After several months, Tom took a turn for the worse. He became lethargic. I decided for his own good, it was time to let him go. I carried him about a quarter of a mile away from the house and released him.

Once free, he perked right up … and started running toward me! He was now free to be a scorpion and I was free to run. I thought he was attacking and had to dodge him, left and right. He pursued me until I disappeared out of sight – and that was the last I ever saw of Tom the scorpion.

Tom was my greatest challenge, far greater than the lizards and black widows. Though his lessons were the harder, they may have been the most valuable. Tom taught me the concept of reciprocal body language. By dancing with Tom, I discovered how to communicate with horses. Our last dance – that frantic dance over the desert sands to escape Tom's raised stinger – taught me that though unusual circumstances might elicit unusual behavior, it is impossible to change a creature's basic nature. Ultimately, a scorpion will always act like a scorpion. Ultimately, a horse can only be expected to behave like a horse.

In the desert, a snake, or insect, or spider, or even a lizard, can deal out serious consequences with its bite or sting. Anything you pick up, turn over, put on, rest on, step on, or open up, if it hasn't been used for a while, may be inhabited by something. The dangers of the desert are hidden.

This concealment causes a heightened awareness in desert people and an almost casual attitude toward the possibility of perilous encounters. In the desert, it is important to always be aware of everything around you. Alertness, following rules and prevention are the best protection.

Between lizards chasing me, black widows protecting my tack and Tom the scorpion stinging me, each encounter had been a lesson in the various possibilities of coexistence. I could not change the nature of my uncomfortable companions. I could only learn what they had to teach me; that coexistence was a function of my conduct, not of theirs ... living this principle leads to the true art of horsemanship.

Chapter X

The Look of Eagles

Appreciation for Nature in Chaos

I developed courage in nature from an experience with the wind in a sandstorm. I would never ask anyone to go through what I went through; never the less, this experience I shared with Mustang gave me a horsemanship skill I could not have acquired through any other circumstance. The sandstorm taught me two things: about Mustang's "look of eagles" and about the power of facing my fears head on.

Growing up, my grandmother taught me to collect and classify the interesting things I encountered on rides. It was during one of these nature rides that the seed of a crazy adventure of my own choosing was planted. I had been taking all day rides for five years now. Long distance rides took preparation since there were so many hidden surprises in the desert.

I always took water and a hat. I packed the saddlebags, one side with lunch and the other side with emergency equipment. I carried a multipurpose tool that could hammer, cut and pry. I took horse-shoe nails, a first aid kit, rope, string, wire, a snakebite kit, halter and lead, sleeping bag, slicker and pillow slip covers I used for saddlebags. I even took a couple test tubes to carry artifacts or rocks or plant samples home for identification.

There are so many surpises out there on the surface of the breathing earth. I might find a stinkbug or a dried remnant of a bush mired in the sand, evidence of an ancient anthill. There might be footprints and holes of animals, broken glass made purple by the sun, ancient annelid shells bleached white from millenniums of time. I might see Indian relics or broken pottery. I could spot an Indian bead from the back of a horse and an Indian camp by the lay of the land.

Some days I rode to the desert sage or to the desert holly or to the smoke trees or to river rock beds at the bottom of the hills. All were half a day's ride from home. I rode ten miles just to see the traveling sand dunes that held no bushes, no holes, no relics – just clean, white sand blown by the wind. The wind piled desert sand as high as buildings, cutting, molding it and dropping it to the earth as from an hour glass, leaving patterns of hills and valleys. The wind left its history in unbroken ribbons, reminding me of the swirls of frosting on my grandmother's devil's food cake.

I wanted to see how the sand formed these patterns in a sand storm. I knew that a sandstorm would be stifling, almost impossible to witness. How could I keep my eyes open to witness it? What would I do with Mustang? The wind would most likely blow him home, but maybe not. I would need eye protection and so would Mustang. We had racing wind goggles for Mustang that protected his eyes from road debris on open trailer rides. I could borrow goggles for myself from my dad's blacksmith shop. I would need a windbreaker, a cap, and a large silk bandana to wear over my nose and ears. I could tie it at the bottom to keep out the sand. I would need gloves. Yes, this would be my next great adventure. If I didn't learn anything about the pattern of the wind, I would at least experience the dunes in a windstorm.

I already knew quite a bit about sand and wind. There is virtually zero visibility in a sandstorm. In a strong sandstorm, I couldn't see my own hand a foot from my face. The wind could strip the paint off a car and clog a carburetor enough to stall an engine. It could pit a windshield and lift the roof off a house as easy as tipping a hat.

I must choose my storm carefully. Storms are funny things. Sandstorms can be seen from miles away. Our desert storms had favorite routes they chose to follow, carrying sand across the desert, dropping it to the earth like an Indian sand painter creating hills and valleys of nothing but sand as far as the eye could see.

I chose an area of dunes at the edge of a storm path. They were not large in breadth or height, not spectacular, but they were close to the ranch, an easy trip. Winds in the desert are such that, if I picked the right storm, I could ride right to the edge of the dunes without a hair out of place, and then ride straight into a huge blow. I anticipated the sensation would be like sticking my head out the window of a car traveling fifty-five miles an hour in a sandstorm.

All of this was speculation, but probably pretty accurate.

It was possible that I would see and learn nothing from this experience. Perhaps I only wanted to feel it. Whatever the reason, I was compelled to do it. Maybe I did it hoping that someone might ask, "What did you do today, Carolyn?" and I could answer, "Mustang and I watched the changing patterns on the surface of the breathing earth like an ocean wave. And yourself?"

As a child, I never missed a sunset. Sunsets were like TV is for children today. Nature was my family, friend and community. I wanted to push myself to find pleasure in an unfriendly environment, to make friends with a desert sandstorm and to confront my fears. I would prove my devotion to the elements and court the winds with my sheer act of being there.

Horses in a windstorm are often unpredictable. The wind made me very nervous as well, but not Mustang. I admired his courage, I felt safe and knew that in that safety I could conquer my fear of the wind.

I told Mustang of my plan and he agreed to the adventure. At the right time, we set out to find my storm. The day was quiet and still. Over the dunes, a big cloud of sand stood out against the sky. I sat on Mustang, waiting for him to choose his course. When he noticed the sand cloud, he held his neck high and readied his muscles for my signal to depart. In a suspended moment in unity, we took off on a beeline to the big white adventure. Mustang paced himself in steady top-speed rhythms of walk, trot and canter. We were out to catch the wind. All the gear we needed for the storm was secured tightly with quick release knots, ready for action.

We came to the edge of the storm after a forty-minute ride. The edge of the storm was a translucent wall of suspended sand kicked up by the wind within. We stepped into the cloud of sand that cut into the daylight and captured a glowing light from the mirrored reflections of the sand particles hanging in the air. I had the strange sensation of entering a body of water. It looked like fog but felt more like a lake. It felt buoyant, even magical!

The air was still and only moved to make way for us. It was thick and seemed to separate to make a path for our progress. I felt like I was floating, no it was stronger than that, a sensation of being lifted up. My mind ran in confused clarity. Here was nature, but not as I was used to it. We headed into its madness or magic. As we rode closer to the blow, the wind whipped up and swept the sand beneath Mustang's feet so that we couldn't see the ground. At the same time, there was no sensation of air even moving a foot above the ground. Mustang walked each step as if not sure where to place his foot on this moving floor. I began to feel dizzy.

Still above and drifting sand below, in suspended disbelief, we watched the riptide of sand racing in slow motion. Running rivers of sand, dry as my breath, flowed around Mustang's feet as he walked. Each step formed a pool of sand as we plodded through the soft rivers, onward toward the heart of the wind.

I stopped and prepared for the big blow. There we were, Mustang with his eye protection and I with not one inch of myself exposed to the elements. Although my goggles were in place, I knew I was kidding myself to think they would keep out the sand. I took to foot; it would be easier to see using Mustang's body as a windshield. I could feel the dust cutting my skin like nettles. My lungs felt thick and the moisture in my body was drawn into the dusty wind like ink being picked up by a blotter. The wind shifted in angry gusts from all directions, trying to ambush us and knock us down.

Luckily, the big blow was less chaotic, but much, much stronger. My vision half gone, my plan was to get on the lee-side of a dune, lay low along the horizon of the dune and see if I could catch a view of the sand being moved by the wind.

At that instant, a wall of wind hit us like a giant wave, slapping the air out of us and stealing the last bit of our ability to control our behavior. I braced into the wind, planting my feet deep into the sand. This only caused me to lose my balance and tumble backwards. I clambered to my feet, only to be blown over again. Holding Mustang's halter rope firmly, I struggled backward into the wind in a peculiar dance, crouching to support myself, then losing my balance, searching for a place that was better than where I was. So much wind, but no air. I gagged and gasped for air. Falling to my knees, I grabbed Mustang's front leg and held on. He turned his back to the wind.

He dropped his head behind me, using my body as a windshield to breathe. There together, we waited for the storm to abate. Sand piled up around me. Every so often, I had to dig myself out and relocate to keep from being entombed. I don't know how long we were out there in the wind, but it seemed like an eternity. By the time the wind finally died down, I had lost all sense of time and direction. In reality, we were only gone from the ranch for a few hours.

When the storm was over, I was a human sandbag. Sand was trapped in my eyes, under my lids, in my eyelashes. I couldn't even feel my scalp – every hair on my body was a sand trap. Even the nails on my hands were lifted up with sand packed under them – but somehow, I had survived the storm.

Mustang weathered the storm amazingly well. He never coughed or showed any discomfort by shaking his ears. Although his goggles worked to a point, he looked like a flounder dipped in flour ready for frying. After many, many showers and baths for both of us, we were almost as good as new. Even so, a week later, I still awoke in the mornings with sand in the corners of my eyes and grit in my mouth.

And nobody asked me, "What did you do today, Carolyn?"

Yet we had danced in the gap to the music of the wind. And the wind had spoken to me of stories found on the surface of the desert floor. The sand moved, the earth breathed, and the sun shone once again. The dunes shifted, markedly defining the wind, lifting like mares' tails in the sky, like spindrift from the top of a wave. The wind appeared to speak of stories through visionary maps, of the patterns defined on the surface of the breathing earth.

The wind had stopped me in my tracks, rearranged me and danced me like a rag doll. I had faced the storm and was not afraid because I was focused on surviving. I had learned how to endure. What I gained from that adventure with Mustang has stayed with me the rest of my life, yet I gained only a part of the quality of spirit that Mustang possessed. Mustang's "look of eagles" had intensified in the wind. I have heard it said and read in books that all who possess this look command respect because they seem to have a deep wisdom that is just out of reach of those who do not possess it. I learned in the sandstorm with Mustang that there is no greater ally than to have personal power in any and all circumstances, a personal power that cannot be shaken.

What I gained from the sandstorm was the knowledge that I had the ability to possess this kind of personal power. Later, I discovered that this personal power could change the attitude of horses around me in a windstorm. They became relaxed and trusting and stayed focused on the tasks at hand. I gained this ability thanks to the windstorm, my interest in nature and Mustang's "look of eagles."

Note: Many years later, during a Seven Step Liberty Training clinic held on Bainbridge Island, Washington, the wind raged for two days, downing many trees around the clinic site. The local newspaper reported winds in excess of 80 miles an hour. I asked the crowd if we should cancel the clinic, but everyone wanted to continue as they were fascinated with the program and impressed with how calm the horses were. The horses calmly learned the seven steps because the bond I shared with them was stronger than the wind. Thanks to an enthusiastic audience that refused to cancel the windy Bainbridge clinic, I discovered I had truly made peace with the wind long ago in a desert sandstorm.

Chapter XI
Rain:
a Thousand Eyes in Harmony
Appreciation of Nature in Harmony

The approaching storm set the stage as the wind and rain set our course. I was riding Mustang a few miles from home. We stopped to watch the desert and listen to the breezes rattling through the dancing chaparral. We were waiting for the coming rain to fill our lungs with the perfume of wet sage. Mustang breathed deeply and snorted into the wind. We took one last look at the horizon, then turned toward home. The rain now fell in blotches and patches as we picked our way back through lights and shadows.

Mammoth shadows raced across the desert floor. Between the sky and earth, the air held suspended curtains of colored lights that looked as if they could be touched as easily as the end of a rainbow. From early morning to afternoon, the sunlight rippled across the valley. Sunlight penetrated the clouds with strobe-like beams traveling over the sand, spotlighting every tree and shrub in their path as I rode. The storm shot music through our veins; Mustang danced as if on puppet strings controlled by the approaching gale. We were alone together in a big, wide world of wonder.

We skirted around the storm to the left and discovered whirlwinds. Desert people call them "dust devils." We moved in and traveled right along with them. The weather was in charge as we played with the whirlwind. Little steps, big steps, short runs, slowing down canters, leaping back and forth – Mustang worked a dust devil like a cutting horse works a cow.

The wind increased, picking up in near gale-force proportions; Mustang and I had to quit playing around. We had stayed out in the storm too long. We took off in earnest, running back to the ranch as the storm overtook us. Mustang's feet hardly touched the ground, partly because he was running for all he was worth and partly because the tail wind was lifting us into the air. He swayed from the winds as he ran. There were moments that we hung suspended in the current of wind as we raced at top speed with the crack of thunder beating us home. I could have been scared to death and maybe I should have been. But I knew at that moment fear was not my friend. The wind increased Mustang's speed beyond any speed that he had ever run. We were being shot forward as Mustang made every attempt to increase the extreme speed we were already traveling. Instead of fear, I was engaged with the same effort as my horse to do whatever it took to get back home.

Reaching home breathless, I jumped off Mustang, gathered up Babe, and we all holed up in the elbow of a ten-foot stack of hay, protected from the brunt of the storm. Still, I experienced the sting of its driving rain, sand, muck and wet alfalfa as we waited, hoping for a greater fury yet to come. In the Coachella Valley, rainstorms are brief, few and far between. They leave in their path balmy weather but with a pleasant chill in the air.

In less than an hour, the storm was gone. The sun reappeared, illuminating tens of thousands of crystalline raindrops left on desert chaparral and residents caught in the storm.

I led Babe to her paddock to dry; Mustang and I walked out to the vineyard. Passing the vineyard on our way out to explore the desert, we saw dormant grapevines bejeweled with huge raindrops hanging from naked canes. The vineyard glowed in the sunlight. Peering through the rows of this enchanted scene, I found crystalline cobwebs covered in droplets. Exhilaration rushed through my veins. I walked through the rows while Mustang grazed contentedly on grasses marinating in rainwater under the bright, gentle sunlight. He tossed his head in the air with every bite, chewing and pulling more grass even when there was no more room in his mouth. His lips shifted, wiggled, tucked, arranged and grabbed at pieces that might be getting away. His teeth ground and chewed as he danced the grasses into his belly.

I plopped down in the wetness and stared face-to-face into a naked cane. I marveled how each raindrop was of equal distance from the other. They were flung haphazardly from the sky, yet now they hung in perfect formation as each held rainbow-captured light. What power to create such harmony from each unique raindrop united perfectly with the next! So geometric, so unified, so planned, so ordered, so marvelous, so easily flung

I gathered up the droplets and flicked them into my hair and tasted the rainwater on the palms of my hands. The rainbow droplets were like fallen stars blown down from the sky.

The desert was taken over by the storm in one frantic battle of wind and rain, and now for a short time dressed in hundreds of liquid rainbows. Like an invitation to a formal ball, I anticipated how beautiful it would be to ride in its sparkling fragrant glory.

I jumped on Mustang to head out into the desert and enjoy the wafting fragrance of the creosote brush and sage that intermingled with the wet sand. I used the mounting style that I learned years ago from Strawberry. I stood over Mustang with his head between my legs. He raised his powerful neck, tossing me onto his back. I felt like Tarzan mounting his elephant, Tantor. Mustang enjoyed tossing me into the air and didn't seem to mind me landing on his back with a splat. As I went about the job of turning myself around, he continued grazing.

After a bit, Mustang grew less interested in eating, becoming content with smaller bites less often, no longer tossing his head. We then struck out into the desert to enjoy the smells, puddles, wadis, singing birds and all nature's reactions and interactions with the abundance the storm had left behind.

All enchanted lands are created by an abundance of water in harmony with need. But no place on earth sings more joyously after a rainstorm than the desert. The air is cleansed, the earth is cleansed and the residents are cleansed. No one is thirsty. Everyone is wet. The many creatures are confused in their joy, having never experienced rain. All creatures burst with activity and celebration for the blessed event of rain!

On our great adventure I wanted to sight birds and other animals sitting out to dry. A big, wet jackrabbit was our first find, sitting beside an equally soaked bush. His fur stuck out in points, gray at the base, black at the tips. He was scratching an ear and then began licking his coat. Noticing our arrival, he adjusted himself for a moment, pausing to think, then thumped the ground and sat perfectly still. He was deciding what to do about our surprise visit. We acknowledged his thump by not looking directly at him, thus giving him more space. He went back to his grooming ritual, and Mustang and I rode on.

Sparrows in the puddles and wadis had not had enough of the rain; they continued splashing and singing with the exuberance that only sparrows have. A lizard, sunning himself on a rock while squinting and blinking madly to dry his eyes, piqued my interest. I could feel myself turning into a lizard as I watched him. While these sun loving creatures appear to have little on their minds, they also appear to be extremely wise. I learned that if I sat still for a while observing lizards they lose their fear and let me pick them up and play with them; they love to play tag. Lizards have very good memories. They remembered me from day to day. After the first encounter, I would not have to wait for them to adjust to my presence to be able to pick one up. John Muir also had an affection for lizards and spoke of how after hours observing and interacting with them, he came to love them. I have heard it is easy to charm a lizard, but I think it is the other way around. They are just special, friendly folks.

After our lizard watch, we saw many animals, most preoccupied with ridding themselves of wet debris. They were a delight to see in abundance, dotting the landscape like garden statuary. Gone was their desire to hide, as if honoring a centuries-old peace treaty reserved for such acts of nature. That afternoon, I saw harmony in diversity and came away appreciating and understanding the importance of the rights of all things on earth.

That evening, lying in bed, I felt in unity with all the creatures that had experienced the desert storm. I could feel the night closing a thousand eyes along with mine.

Chapter XII

Ora Rhodes and the Indio Date Festival

Thank God for Chicken Pox and Humble Pie

There was nothing wrong with the training I had given the horses I was trying to sell to Ora Rhodes. I just didn't know what he was looking for in a horse.

Ora was a friend of my family and a horse trainer in the Perris Valley near Hemet, California. Throughout my childhood, he helped me whenever he came to the desert, which was about three times a year. Ora and I struck up a horse-related friendship through his advice and our business dealings. By the age of ten, I was already producing child-safe pleasure horses that Ora bought from me. During my apprenticeship with Ora, my appreciation of him grew because of the many times he turned down a horse I offered him. He would explain what was wrong with the horse, and I would do whatever it took to fix it. Ora hardly ever told me how to fix the problem; I had to figure that out for myself.

I discovered that what Ora wanted was a horse that would load into a trailer without too much commotion, stop easily from a full run and be able to leave a group of horses when on a group ride. If the horse I offered him couldn't perform these things, I blamed it on the idiosyncrasies of that particular animal. My idea of a good horse was one that saddled easily, didn't buck, run away, kick or bite. To me, these were the marks of a well-trained horse. Ora taught me that producing a good horse was more than training the faults out of a horse; rather, it was the training I needed to put into a horse.

In 1952, Indio started the annual Date Festival and Horse Show. The festival opened my eyes to what I could expect out of a well-trained horse.

The first Date Festival was held in February, the season of wild-flowers, windstorms and shifting sands. Through all the sand-storms, the festival must have appeared to the good citizens of Indio much like a mirage. Its theme was the Arabian Nights and the story of Aladdin's lamp. Its buildings were reminiscent of ancient Baghdad. A stucco wall ten or twelve feet high circled the com-pound. It was brightly painted with turrets meant to hold marching sentinels. A domed tower was adorned in swirls of foiled Maypole colors of gold, purple, deep turquoise green and rust. Lights be-decking the hallways and tower windows suggested a world within those walls.

I lived a mile and a half from the fairgrounds. When the fair opened, I watched spotlights chasing across the sky every night, sending out an invitation to join in the pageant. The pageant began at the stroke of darkness, bursting forth with the tale of Princess Scheherazade. I tried to see every performance.

Everyone came to the pageant in costume and sat under the stars. Audience members participated and had lines to contribute: boos, moans and "Long live the Princess!" which were backed up by a full orchestra, appropriate drum rolls and a horn used for snake charm-ing. Everyone inside those Arabian walls united to tell a story with Aladdin flying through the air on a magic carpet, reciting his words in song. A magic genie appeared in a puff of smoke. Elephants draped in tapestry paraded with camels, monkeys and costumed horses through all sorts of exotic riches: jewels, feathers, fabric, pottery and rugs. Fifty people in exotic costumes along with danc-ers and courtiers rounded out the princess's marriage entourage. It was a time in Indio's history when the imagination and passion of a community shared in a dream, one I shared myself, a dream of the desert song.

I, too, had a part to play. I held my camel backstage while he wait-ed to enter the parade. Behind the stage was a quiet, urgent buzz of action and serious preparation. It was thrilling to have a role and purpose in such a production.

Night after night, the same people came back to enjoy it all over again. If you wore a costume, you got in free. The audience was as colorful as the players on the stage.

Inside the fair I discovered a horse show was to be held. It was a huge Class A show for all events. I had never seen a fair or festival

– or a horse show. I had spent my weekends at the Sheriff's Posse and had competed in gymkhanas. A horse show, I felt, must be similar to a gymkhana. My ego was sitting pretty high those days. After all, my community used me as their local horse trainer. I felt I would be a ringer at the show. Ora respected me and I was counting on him to give me a hand. As it turned out, he gave me no help, other than the entry book he sent me in the mail.

It took all my ingenuity to fill out the forms and find out on my own what was expected. In retrospect, Ora must have thought I had at least seen a horse show and knew my way around. I perused the show catalog, and entered almost every western class offered: western pleasure, working cow, stock horse, reining horse, trail horse, etc. I would have picked all of them, but I figured five or six classes a day were enough for me. Based on my experience at the gymkhanas we had at the Sheriff's Posse on Sunday, I knew I could do it. After all, there was not much running involved.

I read the rules and the requirements of each performance. I had three months to prepare. I felt that was plenty of time. Mustang was a dream of a horse and really put his heart into anything I asked of him. Every day after school I worked him in an oval pattern about the same size as the fairgrounds arena. One of the benefits of living in the desert is that arena size is your choice. I now look at the desert as God's largest dressage court.

I worked at the walk, trot, canter and practiced my stock horse patterns – figure eights, run and slide, stops and spins – which for us looked like twirling around and swooping end over end. None of it made much sense to me. All in all, it was more difficult than I had originally expected, but this boosted my confidence even more. I knew no one else would be able to beat Mustang and me. I would win these classes for sure.

I mastered the jog trot. I wasn't sure of my canter, but it felt good. Our walk was perfect and our figure-eights at the canter were coming along well. My biggest fear was that Mustang had never worked a cow. We would just have to fake it at the show.

A week before the show, calamity struck. I came down with chicken pox and had to stay in bed. No matter how I pleaded, my parents would not let me show my horse. I was devastated; all my dreams were shattered. I just knew I was the best rider in the valley and hated losing all the glory and all the trophies. My parents said

I could go next year. They suggested that maybe I wasn't all that prepared to win at the show. I had never seen a horse show and couldn't argue the point. All I knew is that I was truly miserable.

The fair lasted three weeks. On the last two days, my parents took pity and let me go watch the classes in the afternoon. I had dreamed and lived every class over and over – or at least what I thought the classes would be like. In reality, they were not at all what I expected.

That horse show opened my eyes and helped me understood what Ora was looking for in a child-safe, western, pleasure horse. The first class I watched, the Western pleasure class, was the class I had been most sure I would win. About a hundred and fifty competitors traveled around the show arena, each one was more perfect than the last. If I had entered the arena with my act, I would have stuck out like a sore thumb, disrupting the whole class.

Boy, did I have my work cut out for me. Mustang had a long winter coat and was not sleek and shiny like the other horses. I had not a clue where the bit should fit in his mouth. I used to let it hang about two inches down from the natural corners of his mouth. I knew nothing about taking the bit up to a point that would create a smile or one or two wrinkles at the corners of his mouth. I didn't even know there were western saddles made especially for competition. I had never seen custom-designed show chaps and never dreamed of anyone riding in his best boots unless it was in a parade. I had planned to show in my picnic best. My stirrups weren't even turned enough to fit my natural foot entrance. I thought a bridle path was a trail in a city park for horse and rider. I had no idea it meant removing the hair at the poll with clippers so the bridle would fit neatly. I had hacked a two-inch space for the bridle, but my scissors could not compete with electric clippers for that professional look. The only thing I had right was the show date and my Navajo blanket pad. The chicken pox saved me from a fate I guess God didn't think I needed to experience. I felt truly blessed.

Ora's stock horse class was next. Everyone in the valley knew that Ora was the best bet to win, but I had never seen him ride.

Ora was the first into the arena to work. I had seen spade-bit bridled horses at the Catron Ranch, so I had a taste for the perfect, collected head set. Ora entered the arena on his horse at a walk. Welded deep in his seat, he sat tall. No part of his body moved, and yet he was relaxed. His horse walked into the huge, empty arena with every muscle readied for action. He looked like a time bomb on a short fuse, ready to explode at top speed; instead, he just walked.

Ora showed complete trust in his horse and yet still remained totally relaxed. He asked his horse to pick up a canter and start the figure eight pattern that Mustang and I had been practicing. He cut two perfect circles at a constant speed as fast as possible to look like a full run, while maintaining complete collection, all without a hint of resistance. Ora sat without even a shift in his clothing to show how he communicated with his horse. As relaxed as Ora was, his horse was on fire. I had never seen such union in effort and companionship and such opposite energies expressed at the same time.

The performance was smooth and every step was even, like a metronome for "The Flight of the Bumble Bee." Ora's horse appeared to be on rails; his head never wandered left or right, up or down. The audience roared. Ora was ready to start his run down the long side of the arena, a required part of this performance. At the designated mark, his horse exploded from the figure eight pattern, reaching full speed, it seemed, on his first or second stride. He was like the roadrunner from the cartoons, not like a racehorse, more like a cannon. He had been waiting for this chance, waiting for the take off!

He shot down the long side of the arena as if nothing in the world could stop him. He looked as if he would run right through the arena wall, take down a few buildings and disappear into the desert. At the designated pole at the far end of the arena, he slid to a stop with no movement of the head up or down, left or right, no resistance to the bit, no aids from Ora detectable to the eye. He just shortened in body, lowered his haunches and slid into a clean, straight stop. They stood there like a statue in the park, frozen, never to move again, like a picture hanging in the Cowboy Hall of Fame.

The audience roared again, three thousand people stomping their feet, yipping, whistling and carrying on. I had never experienced this many people in one place making so much noise. It shook me up a little, but the statue down in front didn't even twist an ear.

Watching Ora's flawless performance, I knew what I had to achieve and how far I really was from my goals. I could forget about competing at the Indio Date Festival for awhile. I would not be ready to enter the stock horse class for quite a few years. I have no words to describe the rest of his arena work, which included his spins, because I could not see really what he was accomplishing. I didn't know a horse could move that fast. It resembled nothing of what Mustang and I had worked out together.

The thing I noticed most was the energy I felt while sitting there watching Ora. I suddenly felt clear headed, calm and relaxed. The noise of the audience drifted away like a cloud passing in the sky. Everything grew very still and I, in a dimension of heightened awareness, became acutely aware of my surroundings. Perched there in my seat, I knew that in this state, anything was achievable. I felt Ora and his horse and I were sharing the same awareness. They, too, did not hear the roar of the crowd.

Ora used horse shows and competitions to prove his ability as a horseman, but not to anyone but himself. As a serious horseman, he measured horsemanship by it's own yardstick.

Always my hero, Ora that day showed me a magnitude of horsemanship far over my head. His performance set a new yardstick for me, a new goal. He reset my sights on a level of horsemanship that I knew little about and even less about how to get there.

Steps of growth, I have come to discover, are like a pendulum that swings back and forth. Looking back at my own development, my success at this juncture came in two stages. First, I needed to believe that I was gifted. Next, I needed to discover that I knew nothing. The most important part of my progress and development was realizing that second step: In my mind, I went from being a top competitor to just another little girl who loved her horse.

My experience at the show was a turning point that gave me choices. I could feel demoralized and quit, or I could continue to pursue my dream of becoming a gifted horse communicator. I did not have the magic that day, but I knew it was somewhere inside me. I could feel it in my bones. I did not quit. I was drawn irresistibly to the heightened awareness that Ora and his horse demonstrated. It truly touched me.

Inspiration kept me going. Ora and the Indio Date Festival gave me a huge dose of inspiration and a large serving of humble pie.

Chapter XIII

Footprints in the Sand

A Lesson from Ora

I had been riding with Ora since I was nine. When I was twenty-two, he invited me to stay at his ranch in the Perris Valley and offered me an apprenticeship in training stock horses. In those days, training stock horses was an art. In fact, less was more when it came to cueing the horse with reins and spurs. The horse was never stressed or pushed. Ora asked his horses to learn and perform new behaviors only when they were ready and capable of performing with ease. He encouraged a willing mind and never hurt his horses' feelings or self-esteem. Ora measured his skill by keeping a great horse performing at a high level throughout its lifetime.

I arrived early one morning in the middle of summer when the grass had yellowed in the valley. Walking down to the barn, I found three of Ora's horses saddled and bridled, each tied to his own tree. They looked content and seemed to enjoy standing in the shade. Ora had placed the halters over the horses' bridles then had tied the halter lead ropes to high branches many feet over the horses' heads. This left about a foot of slack in the line if the horse stood directly under the hanging rope. I knew Ora had a reason for doing this, but I wasn't sure what it was.

I inspected the horses closely – fittings and adjustments – and his horses inspected me closely as well. They were alert, relaxed and respectfully curious, reaching with their noses for a possible sniff while remembering to keep the slack in the line. I had seen Ora and many other horsemen tie their horses this way. In fact, I used this method myself, although I didn't know why. I assumed that if it was popular with so many top trainers, it must have some merit. I figured it couldn't hurt to copy old traditions and it made me look like I knew what I was doing when people dropped by my ranch.

I greeted Ora as he came out of the barn and asked him how often he tied up his horses and how long he kept them tied, trying to sound like I already knew the answer. He told me he kept them tied for a few hours a day about five days a week. He volunteered that it developed a quiet, solid disposition in his hot stock horses and took the edge off them, developed patience and taught them not to pull back on the rope.

"A daily routine develops a well-adjusted horse," Ora said.

Even after Ora explained the method, I didn't really get the point until many years later. I eventually realized that this method is an excellent way to help yearlings and two-year-olds develop maturity and manners. It develops a horse that never pulls back and can be tied anywhere while simultaneously training him to properly accept a rein aid from the rider's hand, under saddle. I recommend it highly for all horses in training. I have never found a reason not to use this method and have discovered two positive side effects. First, it develops a horse that will enjoy long trailer rides; second, it develops a horse that doesn't shy when you are riding him. This last benefit may be the strongest reason to incorporate this method in your own training program.

It is important to tie your horse to a tree rather than a pole. The tree offers welcome shade and its natural energy has a good psychological effect on the horse. Introduce this method as a pleasant ritual so your horse never feels uncomfortable or desires to pull back. Initially, you might tie your horse to the tree for only a few minutes a day, gradually increasing the length of time until he builds up his tolerance. I start by tying a horse for only a few seconds and asking him to be patient for that short time. Within a week, he's got it.

Within twenty minutes of my arrival, Ora handed me one of his semigreen bridled stock horses to work out in his large arena. He said to tack her up and start working her, so he could see what I could do. I felt reasonably confident. The horse was a well-mannered five-year-old chestnut mare named Socks. Socks was already being ridden in a spade bit. I have never used this bit myself, but in Ora's skilled hands it was not abusive.

By this time in my life, I was a successful trainer and had won many championships as an all-around rider. I had a prestigious job training at Shadowland in La Jolla, California, a show barn of a hundred and fifty hunters and jumpers. Ora had gotten me that position, so I felt sure I could work with him with dignity, or at least be of use to him.

The only thing I was at all nervous about was how to saddle Socks, because I knew that all trainers have their own right way of saddling. I had inspected Ora's horses that were tied to the tree for just that reason. It really paid off, too, except for one little problem that occurred when I started tacking up the big chestnut mare.

I placed her saddle on where it should be, not too far forward or back. The blanket was just right under the saddle. The cinch was exactly where it should be; however, I apparently made one big error.

When Ora rode by, he announced that the saddle was crooked and advised me to start over. At that point, I knew I was in trouble. The saddle looked straight to me. I saddled and unsaddled Socks, but Ora disapproved of each attempt for a grueling hour until he'd had enough and did the job himself. I could have saddled a string of ten horses in the time it took me to not saddle that one chestnut mare. More than once during that hour I questioned my choice of careers.

Next, I attempted to bridle Socks only to meet with the same dismal result. I did a good job with the process, the adjustments and the fittings, but when Ora walked by, again he scowled. I asked what was wrong. He said, "The bit is not straight in your horse's mouth." Every time he walked by I asked, "How's that?" and he'd answer, "Not straight." He finally got a measuring tape and tried to show me how far off I was. I could not see it. He bridled Socks himself and said, "I'll meet you in the arena."

By then I felt amazed at my lack of perception. This amazement is typical of apprentices in training because of our inflated egos. I should have focused not on my lack of perception, but on Ora's brilliance. Ora was a quiet, polite cowboy who never raised his voice to anyone or anything. When you crossed him, you only got a short philosophical story, or a light-hearted joke, but somehow, it had the same impact as a severe tongue-lashing. I wanted his approval and when I didn't get it, I was crushed.

I entered the arena and began warming up my horse. Ora was quiet – a good sign, I thought. Thirty minutes passed and I felt I had redeemed myself. Suddenly, Ora burst out laughing. He grabbed his hat and looked up at the sky.

"Carolyn! I figured it out – why you have a problem saddling and bridling a horse! It's because you don't ride straight!"

He said my horse went crooked and I didn't sit straight in the saddle, either. He spared my last shred of dignity by adding that I was doing a good job with his horse and that I must be quite talented to get such a good performance out of her, considering I rode so darned crooked (Ora never swore).

There I sat, loping around, trying to adjust myself on Socks to no avail. This went on all afternoon, horse after horse. Like most great horsemen of his day, Ora gave no long explanations or "how-to" instruction. He left the problem squarely in my lap, and offered no advice. In fact, after that, he never brought it up again. It was up to me to solve my dilemma.

I rode crooked for many years. In my defense, so did every other rider in the show ring, and I was still winning handily. But every time I went to pick up my trophy, I could hear Ora reminding me how far I had to go.

One day immediately after the arena had been drug, Ora said, "Let me show you something, Carolyn. If you master this, you won't need all those years of lessons."

He rode his horse at a trot in a straight line through the center of the arena to the far end and then back. He said, "Look at the ground – the footprints."

I looked. As he'd ridden across the arena, his horse's hooves left half-circles in the sand. On his return, his horse had stepped perfectly onto the prints, closing the circles.

Ora then rode in a huge circle at the lope, four times around the arena. His horse left only a single set of footprints in the sand. As he talked to me, he brought his horse down to a walk. The horse's gait made no difference; the result was the same. Each circle he rode was perfect, as if drawn by a compass.

When he finished, Ora rode over to where I was sitting on the fence. He said that until that exercise became simple for me, I had more to learn about collecting a horse and understanding the meaning of straight, because both these elements are essential for a horse to reach his fullest potential.

Ora then rode back to the barn, not even waiting for my response. It was best that way. We avoided confrontation, and we both kept our dignity.

A week went by and I got a call from back home. Something occurred that made it impossible to continue studying with Ora. This was a great loss; however, in the time we spent together, I learned a lot, though few words were ever spoken. What transpired between us in that short time impacted my development as a trainer throughout my life.

When I left, I took Ora with me in my mind. He was always there while I was training in my own barn, watching me, instructing me. When he died, his ghost sat on the arena rail, still offering his dry humor in a few sparse words. I knew one day I would be able to look him squarely in the eye on the subject of straight.

Twenty years later, I finally spoke out loud to him, "I know what straight is, Ora. I know everything about straight."

I had just worked a horse, doing the very same exercise he had shared with me – the exercise I had been practicing diligently for 20 years. As I rode out of the arena, I looked back to see Ora sitting on the fence with a smile on his face, looking at the single set of footprints on the ground behind me.

Did this mean I became as accomplished as Ora? No, never.

No one is as great as the Master.

Carolyn Resnick

Book Three

Educated
by Wild Horses

Chapter XIV

Mustang's Release

Opportunity

I was nine the summer my father got a call from the sheriff's posse. The caller wanted my father's help gathering up some horses the townspeople had pastured on open range land over the summer. Most of our neighbors had pastured their horses for the summer in the San Jacinto Mountains and now it was time to round them up and bring them home. It was late September and the weather had cooled off.

The horses had been turned loose in the pine flats just below Hurky Creek and Hemet Lake on a piece of land used by a movie studio to make western movies. Many Roy Rogers movies had been filmed there.

Roy Rogers was my hero. Every Sunday I attended the movies. The matinee cost fifteen cents leaving ten cents for candy. I can't believe that could be right; perhaps the matinee was twenty cents with five cents left over for candy. Whatever the price, I knew, even then, it was a good deal. The theatre showed cartoons, serials and movies. I went for the western movies, to see the horses.

Other than Roy Rogers, I didn't care a thing for the cowboys. I was very fond of the Indians, though, and rooted for them. Indians rode bareback and used only a little piece of rawhide to control their ponies. And Roy talked to his horses just like I talked to mine. I could tell how much Roy loved Trigger, because he ended his movies by riding off into the sunset after saying something to his horse like, "Come on, boy. I guess it's about time for us to hit the road." He would hold Trigger's face right next to his and pet him with sincere affection. So I fell in love with Roy and that has remained a life-long admiration.

The sheriff's posse called my father because a band of wild horses that belonged to the movie studio had infiltrated the group of horses they had turned loose. The wild horses had influenced the domestic horses, and now they could not catch the domestic horses. For weeks they had tried to round up the horses on foot as they had sent all their horses to pasture for the summertime. They called my dad because we were the only people who had not turned our horses loose in the mountains. My father and I talked about how to get the horses back and he came up with a plan.

Although I didn't know it at the time, rounding up the town's horses with my dad would prove to be the once in a lifetime opportunity that would introduce me to wild horses and change my life forever.

My father knew of both my interest in releasing Mustang back to the wild and learning about wild horse behavior. So he thought up a plan that would fulfill both dreams. We would turn Mustang loose and see if he could influence the herd and take over leadership. If things worked according to the plan, I could then have Mustang lead the herd into a large catch pen and the problem of retrieving the valley's horses would be solved. At the same time, I would get my chance to see wild horses and how they behaved. And Mustang would get his freedom and the chance to prove that he was happier in the desert with me than in his birthplace.

I sure hoped Mustang would live up to his part of the bargain. It was chancy turning him loose to the wild again. But I had to know if Mustang cared for me as much as I thought he did. We had been together for a year. No longer did I need to keep him in a corral. He often had complete freedom on the ranch but when confined, he still looked to the hills and danced.

I kept Babe corralled. If let out at the same time, they probably would have taken to adventurous marauding through the desert. Mustang loved to roam; once, he was gone from the ranch for a week. We looked everywhere for him. And I was afraid something terrible had happened to him. Finally, a neighbor called to say he had him at his place. It turned out that while I was in school, Mustang took off on an adventure without me. He returned to one of the private spots we enjoyed together on our afternoon rides.

The neighbor owned a pig farm that lay unattended during the week. I am not proud of this, but when we discovered this unattended pig farm, we knew we could have the time of our lives chasing the pigs. Mustang told me that he could jump the fence, but we just raced up and down, chasing the pigs back from the fence. Soon, however, we had worked ourselves into a frenzy. One thing led to another and before I knew it – well, the fence was only three feet high. We just, like sort of, well… jumped in.

Chasing those pigs was one of our grandest adventures, and I saved it for special occasions. We only did it once in a great while because I knew it was wrong, wrong, wrong to trespass and harass the pigs; moreover, it was very dangerous and possibly an inhumane act.

Mustang gave away our secret by going there and chasing pigs on his own. I got grounded for a month, and I grounded Mustang to a month of corral life. We never went over there again. I learned very well that if I was going to continue to ride alone, anything that happened was my responsibility, my fault. I had to be in charge and aware of the consequences of my acts. I had been allowed too much freedom. I also learned that grounding works as well with horses as it did with me.

We both stayed completely away from the pigs from that day on. Mustang and I took to long desert rides, staying clear of other people's property. After the pig incident we went back to enjoying the desert as our main recreation. My bond with Mustang grew even deeper from our solo trips into the desert looking for unusual topography. There was a place where the desert's topography supported no life and looked like craters on the moon. No one ever went there. Out there we discovered a freedom that didn't exist anywhere else on the planet. Mustang was different out there. He lost interest in watching for predators. I could tell he liked our visits as much as I did. We enjoyed together what the desert had to offer and shared the same thoughts and feelings. We knew the smell of the desert rain came from the mesquite, creosote and desert sage; we knew that dust devils were fun to dance with; we knew being together was what made everything come alive.

Now we were facing our greatest challenge, to separate the town's horses from the mustang herd. In all domestic horses lives a wild horse, and in all wild horses lives a domestic horse; that was my theory and I was getting a chance to prove it. The first part of my theory was already clear: The domestic horses were happy and healthy surviving in the wild. It was up to Mustang to prove the second part, that he truly enjoyed domestication as he knew it.

I remember feeling nervous riding up to the pasture where we would release Mustang. My dad wasn't much help as he pulled the trailer up the road. Periodically, he broke out in Wild Cat Kelly's song, "Don't Fence Me In."

After a grueling 20 miles we came to our destination, turning onto a dirt road that headed up into the backcountry. The road traveled through rolling hills, mountains, rocks and pine trees. We reached the furthest point that a truck and trailer could pass. This is where we would release Mustang. Dad stopped the truck, walked back to the horse trailer and unlocked the tailgate. I helped lower the gate to the ground, took Mustang's tail in my hand and asked him to back out of the trailer.

Mustang backed out and jerked his head around to look at his strange surroundings. With the wild look I had seen before, that "look of eagles," he whinnied with all his might, his belly jerking with anticipation. Not wanting to prolong the agony, I reached up and undid his halter. I expected him to race off and explore this land that had the power to ignite memories of his once-wild existence. To my surprise, he slowly turned and looked in every direction. Even so, I expected that at any moment he would stampede away and never look back. Instead, he took to grazing, strangely hanging very close to us. We waited there with him for a while, sitting on the fender of my dad's '49 Ford truck, eating a brown bag lunch my mother had prepared for us.

When my dad finished his lunch, he took the lunch bag, blew it up and popped it. He was hoping the loud bang would chase Mustang off to freedom. Mustang didn't react. He was at home with us in the wild! The first essential ingredient for our plan to work was there: Mustang did in fact, through and through, accept the bond I believed we had.

I walked up to Mustang, repeated the story of why I was leaving him to these lands and told him goodbye. I said I would return soon and for him to wait. I gave him a big kiss. He stood there and watched us leave.

As we started back down the road, my father said, "Carolyn, that horse of yours better stay in those hills. As much as he loves you, I worry he will try to come home."

When my dad was a kid, he'd had a horse named "Dolly." Dolly was a cute Morgan mare and my dad had worshipped her. Because of her beauty and composure, Dolly got a job in a movie, The Iron Door. I don't know all the details, but once she was loaned to a family that took her miles away from my father. Her first night away from home she broke the fence down. Coming home on the old "Jackrabbit Trail," a two-lane highway, she was hit by a car and killed.

So dad was worried, but we both knew Mustang was a different horse. He would never panic and he was car wise. Besides, he had spoken to me with his eyes when I left him, telling me he would wait for me. My biggest worry was how Mustang would handle his first night alone.

The wind whistled through the cracks in the side window of the old Ford truck as I listened for Mustang's call. My dad and I sat in silence. The distance increased mile by mile. Mustang and I had never been so far apart. I felt empty inside. My mind wandered back to the first time Mustang and I had met.

My father had found Mustang for me and paid two hundred and fifty dollars for him. He told me, "If you don't like him, maybe the owner will return my money."

As I took Mustang's reins and started to mount, I had a good feeling about him instantly. He felt good to sit on and after five minutes, I was absolutely convinced that Mustang was the horse for me – and now, I might never see him again. He might get hurt in the wild or trying to return home to me.

My father read my thoughts. He told me he had no doubt that Mustang was perfectly safe out there. He said that Mustang's attachment to me would not be challenged and that I was only feeling lonely. He said, "Trust me. I knew he was your horse even before you did."

After several weeks, we went back to check on Mustang. We found him easily, not far from where we left him. He was happy and healthy. His new life in the wild had not changed him. He still remembered me. The wild horses had not impressed him with the fear of capture.

My father was eager to discover Mustang's role in the herd. He wanted to see if Mustang had infiltrated the herd and established his dominance over them. We both knew that Mustang would not accept any other position, but we worried that his size might get him hurt in dominance fights with larger horses. We also knew that he had to succeed in taking over as leader for our plan to work.

My dad didn't want me to ride Mustang or spend too much time with him on our visits. We had to peek around branches, trees and rocks as we viewed his progress with the other horses. On our first visit, we learned that dominance wasn't coming easily, but it was coming. Mustang's smaller size really was a problem, but his desire was strong. I saw him lose several skirmishes with a couple larger geldings, but Mustang was quick enough not to get hurt and his endurance in returning argument over land and grass issues was relentless. He was smart. I watched him pick fights over things that didn't much matter to the other horses. He seemed to know he could win an argument that his opponent didn't have a strong opinion about. Once, we saw him spend the whole afternoon squabbling over almost anything. The other horses started giving him room just to have peace.

After the second visit, we knew all the stories we'd heard about Mustang being a great leader were true. He was taking over not due to his size, but because of the extreme endurance he had built up from our desert travels together. In observing the herd's pecking order, I realized that the lead horse was not necessarily the strongest, but always the horse with the greatest focus.

I shared my observations with my dad. I told him that Mustang's desire for leadership was greater than that of his rivals and that his focus was more enduring. He wisely replied, "Let that be a lesson to you, Carolyn. If you want something in life, know what it might take to get it, and accept nothing else."

The rest of the way home, I reflected on the broader aspect of the experience of Mustang's release. The sheriff posse had no idea of how we planned to catch the horses, and I had no idea of how important it was to my life that the sheriff's posse horses had become impossible to catch. The experience my Dad set up was the turning point of my life, taking me in a direction I longed to experience. My Dad arranged the event of catching the horses using Mustang so that Mustang could express his masterful abilities of leadership.

What took place next was magical.

Chapter XV

Mustang' Return

Don't Fence Me In

My dream of returning Mustang to the wild and observing wild horse behavior had its price. Six weeks without Mustang was a long time for me and I was glad that we were now going to bring him home. Telepathic communication was feeling natural to me, probably due to my need to reunite with Mustang. Long before we arrived at Mustang's drop off spot, I was sending him messages of our return.

Dad stopped the truck at the spot we had released Mustang. I jumped out and gazed across the valley, searching the panorama for Mustang. As my eyes reached the grasslands, there he was just above the meadow on a lookout point.

He began his descent like a stag, stepping sure-footed over the craggy rocks. He threaded a path through brush and unseen footing, making his way down to meet me. Leaping over the last few feet of rugged terrain, he entered the meadow at a canter with measured stride. Mustang had anticipated my arrival.

We met in the center of the meadow and Mustang circled me, bounding and leaping sideways like a young colt playing with his shadow. His exuberance told me of his adventures in the hills and how much he had missed me, how glad he was for my return, how happy he would be to go home with me and how he looked forward to seeing Babe. He circled one last time, sidling up to me and dropping his arched neck over my shoulder. He cradled me between his shoulders and head, almost touching me completely in his embrace without touching me at all. I held his head against my face, lost in the moment.

My dad and I had headed out before sunrise. We figured it was going to be an all-day project – but what I saw next made it look like we'd figured wrong. The rest of the herd were making their way down the hillside toward us. I was excited to see our plan working; I was even more excited to see the answer to all my questions: Did I have a right to keep a wild creature of God in captivity? Was I wrong to ask him to serve my wants and needs?

When I turned him loose, Mustang could have chosen to join the wild horses or return to his original home only fifty miles to the west. But he had waited for me. Neither time, nor distance, nor his own wild nature could sever the bond between us. It was a good test to see if I had the right to keep Mustang in captivity.

I lay down in the grassy field and Mustang stood watch over me. I looked up at the blue sky and slow-moving clouds as we both waited for the rest of the horses to join us. Mustang looked at me, snorted, then shook his head at the approaching horses to set his boundaries and show them how much he was willing to share of the territory he and I had claimed together.

Lying there, I could hear the other horses approaching, the ones just entering the meadow and the ones making their way down the rocky hill. I could hear their footsteps in the grass. I could hear horses discovering my presence and communicating this discovery to the others with erratic steps and astonished snorts. I could hear the contented sounds of horses grazing.

I rose slowly, keeping my back to the horses so as not to alarm them. Mustang and I walked out along the edge of the meadow, then continued down into the valley that held the catch pen. Six weeks earlier, when we had released Mustang, I had closed the gate. As we approached, I could see evidence that the herd had been grazing the edges of the fence line. The interior of the five-acre pen was now covered in tall, green grass. When the townspeople had first tried to catch their horses, the catch pen had been over-grazed, giving the horses no reason to enter what was obviously a trap.

I worked fast to avoid arousing the herd's suspicion. I had to open the gate before the first horse had a chance to get down to where we were. The gate was huge! It was made from four fence posts set about six feet apart from each other. Five strands of barbed wire connected these posts. One end gatepost was fastened by barbed wire to one of the strong end posts of the permanent fence. The other end of the gate was held by barbed wire loops connected to the top and bottom of the other permanent end post. I worked frantically on the taut barbed wire top loop that held the gate closed. When it finally released, the gate recoiled like a stretched spring. I quickly dragged the twenty-foot section of gate open. Mustang had already entered the pen and was grazing. The trap was set with a seal of approval from Mustang. He was having the time of his life grazing on a perfect pasture. I sat next to the downed gate to hide and waited.

Following Mustang, the horses entered the pen in groups, rushing through the gateway as if they had discovered a secret pass. I had based my plan on the old proverb: "The grass is always greener on the other side of the fence." In this case, the grass really was greener on the other side and the plan worked to perfection. I had figured we'd be there all day gathering the horses but it was still morning. In a short time all the domestic horses had worked their way into the pen. It was like separating the yolk from the white of an egg. The town horses went in easily, but the wild horses recognized the pen as a trap and would have no part of it. They stayed outside, grazing here and there and left the lush field to horses with less savvy.

Closing the gate was not easy. I had no turn back person or anyone to hold up the middle section of fence. I had to work alone, because anyone else approaching the herd might scare them back out of the field.

The herd accepted my connection to Mustang and was reassured when they saw their leader was not afraid of me. Even so, I moved slowly so as not to alert the herd to the closing of the gate. I maneuvered the gate section by section, inch by inch, into a closed position in the bottom loop, stopping whenever a horse chose to look my way. Somehow I managed to get the fence in an upright position, a precarious pretense that the gate was in place.

Near the end of my task, a couple people from the Sheriff's Posse moved in quickly to help, one pulling the fence taut and the other battling the barbed wire top loop over the gatepost. As soon as they showed up, the wild horses took off and the domestic horses started running in the five-acre pen looking for a way out, but to no avail. I had done it!

I had done what no one else could do although they'd tried and tried. Everyone figured my Dad and I would have to ride out and catch the horses, or else rely on some trick up our sleeves, or a cun-

ning plan derived from years of experience. Many people later told
me they doubted my dad and I could do it. They thought we might
even have to borrow the neighboring Sheriff's Posse to round up
the horses.

My father, however, figured I could do it myself with the help of
Mustang … and he was right.

The rest of the day was devoted to a barbecue. It was a lot like the
barbecues we would have at a cattle round up. Lots of grown-ups
and kids joined together, eating and having fun. The town folk had
come along to try to round up their own horses, if my dad and I
were unable to get the job done.

Over thirty horses had been turned loose at the beginning of
summer and not one was missing. All the kids got a horse to ride.
I jumped on Mustang without bridle or saddle, and we all set out
to play in the wide-open countryside, singing "Don't Fence Me In."
This was my day to shine.

Everyone in the valley had their day to shine; it was a sort of pact
our community made with itself. Every person contributed something special to the community. My dad was the problem solver. My
mother was the theme party planner and reported on the doings of
our "Los Chinocos" club for the local newspaper. Abe Abersol was
the community director. My best friend, Myrna, was the artist. Bill
Clause was the strongest kid in town. Even as children, we all had
honorable titles, we each had a unique service to offer to our community. We grew up together without a reason to compete, because
each and every one of us was needed in a special way.

I looked at this day as a public graduation, an acknowledgment
that I had a skill on which the community could depend. I was
the "horse girl" that talked with the animals. My community had
identified my purpose. It felt good to be needed by my family and
friends, but it felt better to be needed by my community. It was a
validation of what I had to offer. I lived in a community that cared
for individuals and among individuals that cared for their community.

That day, the community gave me my voice. They planted a seed
that slowly grew. With Mustang home, I knew right then that I would
be an eternal student of the ways of horses and communication.

Chapter XVI

Silent Horse

Vision Quest

In the early fifties as I was growing up, children's willingness to try to solve their problems earned a lot of respect from most folks. There was a different mentality in that era. Most parents realized that practical experience shaped character better than advice. People had a different opinion of how to support family and friends. If you wanted help, you needed to ask. I was taught that before seeking advice, I needed to consider who would be the best person to ask and not bother anyone else with my problem. My family felt that too much advice and support weakened character.

My mother was careful not to shape my opinions with her own. When I was eight, I remember putting on a navy blue and white, narrow, horizontal-striped top with pants that had wide green and white, perpendicular stripes. I didn't know it at the time but I looked like a jailbird. I asked my mother for her advice and approval of what I was wearing. I commented proudly "Look what I am wearing. I think it is a perfect match! What do you think?" She replied simply, "If you like it and are comfortable in it, it is fine!" She allowed me my own thoughts and feelings to develop me as an individual.

On that particular day, I was dressing up for a portrait with Mustang and my father's horse, Flashlight. My mother allowed me to choose what I wore. When I got older, I was horrified with that photo. Today it is my very favorite. I remember what I was thinking when the picture was taken. I thought I looked fabulous. I remember to this day how thrilled I was to be able to orchestrate the photo, from the clothing I chose to wear to how I wanted my picture taken. I have a great ability to remember much of my life growing up. I owe it to how my family raised me. If my mother had told me how to dress, I doubt if I would have remembered anything about that day.

The formula my parents used was a balance between practical experience and advice measured out appropriately. They felt that practical experience was a better teacher than being spoon fed information, because children never forget lessons learned through practical experience.

My family guided me toward experiences that would lead me to the right decisions in life. They developed my respect for family values. When they offered me help and advice, I was always eager for their direction.

After my experience rounding up the horses with Mustang, my parents looked into the possibility of me being able to study the wild horses. A couple days after the roundup, my parents told me that they had received permission from the movie studio for me to spend my summer vacation on their land with the wild horses.

The edge of the land was only a few miles from my parents' cabin. The days my parents were at the lake, I could be with the wild horses. Hemet Lake was just across the road. I could spend mornings with the horses, have lunch with my parents and return to the horses in the afternoon.

When I learned of my good fortune, I revisited the spot where we had corralled the domestic horses. I spent that day focusing on my plans for the summer with the wild horses. Through my grandmother's influence, I felt the answers to all my questions about the wild horses would come from the land itself. She suggested I go on a vision quest to look for a spot in the wild horse habitat that had a sacred feel, like what I might imagine an American Indian would find sacred. She said I would recognize the spot when I found it. It would have magnetic energy. I was to wait there for a vision to reveal the direction I needed to follow if I was to learn the language of the wild horses and gain their trust. She said that I could use my imagination to guide the way.

Everyone agreed that my grandmother was the smartest member in our family. They said she was wise because of her years, her education and her natural intelligence. They told me that she had a profound understanding of what was important in life. My grandmother was my greatest influence as a child. She guided my understanding and appreciation of nature and how to use nature as a classroom. She guided me into the world of nature, knowing it would develop my knowledge and intuition.

Her passions in life were the natural sciences and mathematics. In college, she majored in botany, astronomy and mathematics. She minored in language and biology. She graduated summa cum laude from Mount Holyoke and was valedictorian of her class. She used her education in the life sciences to search for the magic in nature and develop formulas for how everything in nature worked and fit together.

When my parents dropped me off at the wild horse range land, my goal was to develop a plan to connect with the wild horses. With my grandmother's advice fresh in my mind, I started walking across the land not knowing what I would find. I had barely started my journey when I discovered the land held breathtaking panoramic views that I had seen in the old western movies. This land was big; its rugged terrain hid ravines and valleys and yet everywhere I looked, I saw trees, rocks, plants, hills, paths, meadows, ridges and animals. Breezes, changing temperatures, riparian zones, mesas, forests, mountains, rock and manzanita surrounded me. Trails and paths crisscrossed the ground, stretching across the landscape through sun and shadow. I could cover great distances on shaded forest trails. Grazing land was everywhere. I walked across beaten down grassland and lush green meadows, then over pine bark and needles fallen from tall pine trees with patches of blue peeking through their branches. Then the ground under my feet changed to dusty gray dirt only to become a sandy floor with open skies overhead. This was truly a land of variety and abundance.

It was a wonderland of nature. I heard my own footsteps. I heard birds flying by, "Feou - feou - feou," their songs making my footsteps lighter. I heard the breeze in the tall grass like chimes. I heard the wind in the tall pines, like creeks and rivers.

I felt like Goliath – strong enough to walk around the world. I, too, could now run with the wind like a horse. The desert sands had held onto every step I took, but here the ground sprang like a trampoline under my feet.

I stepped into a circular meadow surrounded by giant pines and rock outcroppings. I found myself in a green sea; strange clumps of grass grew so tall they swooned to the earth like daffodil stalks in autumn. Breezes ebbed and flowed, wafting through the blades of fresh, green grass. Broken pine branches littered the meadow. Rich, brown pinecones of every variety decorated the clump grass like resinous jewels.

I chose a spot where I could see the entire meadow. Everything around it was beautiful and harmonious. The pinecones scattered so randomly seemed arranged purposely to delight the eye. Pleasant breezes created the refreshing coolness of spring. Even the rocks had the esthetic balance of a Japanese garden. It's exquisite beauty moved me deeply; I knew I had found my spot. This place held great power and knowledge. It seemed like an ancient sanctuary, a spot chosen as sacred by other people long before me. I knew this place would yield the key to unlock the door to the secret society of horses.

I sat and waited. A reverence crept over me as I sat on the meadow's edge under the giant pines. I imagined an Indian had entered my spirit. I could feel war paint upon my face. I could feel different Indians inside my body. They came and went, but one, in particular, resonated louder than the rest.

He stood before me, a young man. I could see no winters upon his face. He appeared to me to be the spirit of an Indian brave. The fringes of his doeskin leggings outlined his strong, erect posture. He spoke to me silently with his eyes and body gestures. I named him Silent Horse.

Our energies flowed from our bodies into the earth and there met and twined together like the roots of the grasses around us. Without words I told him I was looking for a key that would make it possible for me to become part of the herd and eventually the leader of these wild horses.

Happy and lighthearted, Silent Horse showed me how he could run with the wind, how he could run between the wind, how he could hide from the wind. He taught me how to hide from the wind. He taught me a heightened awareness and how to keep it. I ran with him; he took my hand and we left the meadow. I learned to run so the earth gave to my touch and twigs no longer broke beneath my feet.

Silent Horse gave me a shove. I caught my balance and looked around me. Just as quickly as he had appeared, he now vanished. In that instant, I knew I would spend my summer on foot. Mustang

would have to stay home with Babe.

My imagination then turned to horses. I imagined I was many horses – old ones, strong ones, weak ones, young ones, brave ones, wise ones. They all differed in their responses to the world, but they all shared the same expressions of movement in their bodies. I discovered universal movements of a silent language, a ballet of energies, a body language in full sentences, a language essential to all animals that must stay on silent watch, using the herd and speed to survive.

As I walked in my imaginary horse body, I no longer had my own feelings. I felt like a horse walking in a new territory; every step I took was another point of view. I came across a creek with a difficult approach; it had carved itself a bed much lower than the grassland through which it flowed. Grass grew down to the creek bank to the very edge, overhanging crusty strata of black soil, then small rocks, pebbles and sand. Watercress and snake grass at the water's edge waved at me suspiciously from just below the water's surface.

Peering closely, I noticed water skippers, frogs, mosquito fish and a few scary boulders scattered in groups along the creek's edge like small families of brown bears lapping water from the crusty bank. I started to notice small details, keeping a soft eye on watch for predators lurking along the creek bank.

I picked my way to a spot that appeared safe and lowered my horse neck, reaching first with my nose, then with my poll, followed by my crest. Slowly, with flexible grace, I reached the cool water. With splayed legs, I drank from a choice spot of uncrossed water, picking the very best top water just beneath the surface.

This was the beginning of my lessons in communication. To be as observant as a horse is difficult, but therein lies the ability to speak in silent tongues.

From this day, getting to know the land and having the vision quest through my grandmother's guidance, I found a plan. I would need three summers to learn about the secret society of wild horses. The first year, I would watch them. The second year, I would interact with them. The third year, I hoped to ride them through a bonded trust.

I was now ready to begin my quest into the land of wild horses. I could hardly wait to tell my grandmother about Silent Horse. When I reached my grandmother's Spanish bungalow, I was not surprised to see more that half a dozen Indians on her front porch. My grandmother knew almost all the Native Americans in the valley. She helped them fight to save their land in Palm Springs so that it could never be taken away from them. My whole family loved Native American people and their culture.

I found my grandmother in the dining room teaching a lesson. When she finished her lesson and heard my story, she said, "You see, young lady, nature is as enchanting as your imagination!" She then added, "If we had never seen a bird fly, we may never have wanted to fly ourselves and consequently may never have invented the airplane." She usually had the last word and it was often some new insight for me to consider. I would take it to heart and think long and hard about what she had said.

Not only did my grandmother's guidance help me to formulate my vision quest on how to approach the wild horses, it also served as a catalyst in helping me plan how to communicate with the wild horses in their own habitat. She had taught me how to think like a scientist and find hidden knowledge that I was not expecting to find. She had taught me that compiled information could be used over and over in different circumstances to reveal new facts. From my vision quest, I learned that my childhood game – pretending that I was a horse – gave me a much better understanding of horses. My imaginative game taught me more than any animal behavior expert ever could. My vision quest also taught me that in each imagined horse that took over my body, there was a common thread in their movements and body language, a universal language, shared and understood by all horses. I learned as well that horses' attitudes are always expressed in their body language and that they could never hide how they felt about me.

I also realized that if I was going to learn the language of the wild horses and get them to accept me into their herd, I could not be riding Mustang. This time he would not be able to help me. Mustang would influence my interaction with the wild horses. I needed to bond with the wild horses on my own and on foot. Even though I knew it would take me longer, I also knew that the more time it took the more I would learn and I was hungry for all the time I could get.

This day and my grandmother's guidance armed me with a plan. I was more than excited and more than ready to follow my quest. into the land of wild horses.

Chapter XVII

The First Summer

Finding My Inner Compass

Tall pines, buttes, mountains … without Mustang.

My first weeks in "the land of wild horses" were memorable, not because of the horses, but because of their absence. My parents did not give me free rein to wander all over the wilderness looking for the herds. They wanted me to get to know the land first, so I wouldn't get lost. I had strict instructions to stay where I could be easily found. The five thousand-acre property was privately owned, posted and patrolled. I was to check in with the patrols. Even though my parents were just across the road at Hemet Lake, I was to restrict my travels to a small area that included the entrance to the property and the main dirt road to the interior. This made it impossible to connect with the horses.

I would connect with the herds eventually, but for now, I savored the distance between us. The woods were enchanting and invited me to get lost in them, but that was exactly what I didn't want to do. I barred from my mind fears of snakes, cats and bears, because, in reality, they lived higher in the mountains and were rarely seen at these lower elevations. My one real fear, one that my parents instilled in me, was the fear of getting lost. They pointed out that while nobody sets out to get lost, it happens quite often. And it could happen to me in an instant, they said, when I least expected it.

I was never afraid of getting lost in the desert because I could see where I was going and where I'd been. I also had a tremendous sense of direction – though I'd never paid much attention to it. Besides, it's nearly impossible to get lost on horseback simply because horses know the way home and will take you there if you give them free rein.

Often, when Mustang and I headed home, I'd give him the reins and let him choose the route. Sometimes he followed the trail we were on; sometimes he took shortcuts. His route was always direct, the shortest path home. He had a built-in compass, memory and a keen sense of using trails, even those left by wild animals.

Now, however, I was in unfamiliar territory and on my own. Because of my parent's restrictions, I started familiarizing myself with my immediate surroundings. I explored the woods and began to memorize the paths and trails. I wanted to be able to find my way home blindfolded.

The forest was actually an array of environmental sections created by timbering practices. A section might cover only a few acres. One section might be a grove of older trees. Another would boast an entirely different variety of trees and saplings. In the deepest part of the woods, I discovered meadows, each with its own characteristics, easily distinguished from the others. The environmental zones seemed to run in connective links with abrupt changes between them. I began to see a pattern to the land, that the sections followed each other in a predictable order, creating a mapped pathway through the wilderness. I figured this map would help me know where I was and where I was going.

I explored everything in detail. I started to "shop" the forest like a curious animal, looking for nothing in particular. With each discovery, I felt a deeper appreciation for the environment. I collected moss from fallen branches, to give to my mother for her flower arrangements. I found deer paths and dung markings and listened to the echoes of the jays on the shifting breezes.

Though I delighted in the forest pathways, I knew I would need something more than the environmental chain to keep my bearings. If the wild horses led me into unfamiliar territory, I could still get lost. I needed the skill Mustang had for knowing how to get home. I decided I could acquire this skill through my powers of observation.

I had heard that Native Americans used landmarks as guideposts in their travels. It occurred to me that I could use the same technique to blaze my own trails. If I paid close attention to the outstanding topographical features of an area, I could find my way back by remembering them.

This did not work. On my return trips, my landmarks had either vanished, changed appearance, or multiplied, making it impossible for me to know which I should follow. So I tried marking my trails. I set cross-sticks, piled up rocks and tied bits of rag along my path to show me the way home. This did not work, either. I couldn't trust my own markers.

I knew about compasses, moss growing on the north side of trees, how to follow riparian zones downhill and how to read the lay of the land. But a compass was of no use when canyons or impassable chaparral blocked my path. The sun was useless on a cloudy day. Moss was unreliable. The riparian zones were too far apart. As for the lay of the land, many places I couldn't read the lay of the land because of the dense trees.

I was on the wrong track. My powers of observation were never going to get me back from the far country where the wild horses roamed. Mustang hadn't relied on landmarks to navigate his way home. I needed what he had. I needed an inner compass that would free me to these lands.

I stopped looking for a solution and went back to experiencing the moment. My grandmother believed that if she was looking for an answer to a problem, the solution would naturally present itself. She told me that nature holds the solutions to all our questions. She taught me to tap into nature by connecting with the moment while waiting for the answer to magically appear. She told me that if you focus on the web of life, which connects all things, it will guide you. I knew if I allowed my subconscious to connect with the land, to relax and enjoy what the day had to offer, the woods would provide the solution to my dilemma.

The scent of the pine forest rose on the air with the morning dew. I caught a faint trace of my solution mingling with the perfume of the woods. I journeyed deeper into the forest, peering through corridors of trees and patches of sunlight. I came to a clearing. Downed trees lay scattered on the forest floor like oversized furniture in a mountain inn. Patches of earth were alive with ants marching, crawling, pulling and tugging their treasures over dry pine needles. The needles made a neat mat under my feet but hampered the ants' passage and progress. Still, they marched with determination. A squirrel chattered his disapproval of my arrival. Light glittered from a dragonfly's wing. It darted forward and hovered, reflecting sunlight in rainbow colors of blue, purple and green.

I remembered a Shakespeare poem my mother taught me, and I

replied to the dragonfly and the squirrel:

> Where the bee sucks, there suck I;
> In a cowslip's bell I lie,
> There I couch when owls do cry:
> On the bat's back I do fly
> After summer merrily:
> Merrily, merrily, shall I live, now,
> Under the blossom that hangs on the bough.

The squirrel did not stop to listen, and the dragonfly flew on into the forest, leaving only the memory of its beauty behind. But its beauty compelled me to follow and to chase the dragonfly. Thin mountain air rushed into my lungs as I tracked it, and the heavy summer perfume started to slow me down. My energy was draining. Nothing seemed necessary or important. I picked a spot and rested. Nestled in the sway of a fallen tree, I fell into a deep sleep.

Half awake and swaddled in dreamy drowsiness, I noticed gnat-like insects dancing in slanted beams of misted light that sifted through the tall pines. They hovered in the brightness, then vanished into the shadows, only to return again. They interacted with each other in a peculiar way. A dance. A jostle. A drama. Perhaps a game or a ritual. Whatever they were doing, it intrigued me. Mesmerized, I lay there watching them for nearly two hours.

I slowly became conscious of the sound of bees buzzing. They were honeybees, coming to life as the sun warmed their world. I realized there was a hive nearby. There they were – in my tree! How had I been so oblivious? This could have been a terrible mistake. Hundreds of bees just a few feet away. I had not been stung.

And suddenly, I had the answer! I saw my solution in the language of the bees. My grandmother taught me that bees dance to inform other bees of nearby pollen. Hovering in place, a bee measures out distance by the number of wing beats, then spins to specify direction.

I would base my inner compass on the bees' dance. Every step I took into the wild would be a remembered choreography like the bees' dance. The dance, played backward, would be my way home.

All afternoon I practiced retracing my footsteps. Perceiving my movements as a dance, it was easy to remember my way back from places I'd never been. I would travel a small distance into a dense forest and then turn around and come back out. Retracing my path became easier and easier. Before long, it became so natural that I wondered why I hadn't thought of it myself, without the help of the bees. Now I was ready to head out into the big country, without Mustang, to "the land of wild horses."

Carolyn Resnick

Chapter XVIII

The Secret Society of Horses

My Acceptance

The wild horses above pinion flats had been collected from many herds across the country and brought together to serve Hollywood's cinematic needs. Separated from their families, they colonized into a true community; over time they had created unified bands within the herd. These horses were more clever than their wild counterparts in other parts of the country. Their experiences with Hollywood filmmakers who used and abused them for Western movies had taught them that humans were predators and that distance was their only protection.

The horses' treatment at the hands of the movie industry had intensified their instinctual flight or fight responses. Playing the stampeding herd so often in Westerns had turned them into ego-crazed runners. Winning their freedom so many times had deeply imprinted on their minds that running was a good thing. It had also developed in them a desire to run just to show off.

I have never since met wild horses as skilled at self-preservation. These herds lived in cat country, but from my observations in summers to come, the mountain lions learned to live on something besides horseflesh. I did not notice any loss of healthy horses in the three summers I spent with them. I imagine that if a cat was foolish enough to pounce on one of these renegades, he'd get the ride of his life, then be flung to the dirt and stomped to death by the rest of the herd. These horses truly understood the power of stampeding, whether it was away from a problem or right over the top of it.

It wasn't going to be easy to study the wild horses. I, too, had been seen as the enemy when I locked the domestic horses in the catch pen with Mustang. I knew they would hold this transgression

131

against me and stampede at the first hint of my presence.

After the roundup of the town's horses, the wild horses had moved further away. It was weeks before I caught even a glimpse of a horse. I had no idea where to find the herds; I only knew that they were somewhere on a rangeland of over hundreds of acres of hills, valleys and canyons. My constant search eventually led to a few chance encounters, but these accidental meetings just encouraged the horses to make a greater effort to avoid me. If I was walking one direction, they were surely running in the other. The more I threatened their invisibility, the more I found myself pursuing mirages of running horses that faded into empty hills, woods and canyons. The only proof of their existence was the dust that lingered in the wake of their flight.

I started to feel a yearning to be with the herd. I felt lost, like a single horse searching for others like himself. Everything seemed to hide the wild horses from me, even the wind and the chaparral. I saw that my search was scaring the horses further and further away.

I stopped looking for the horses and started looking for signs of them. Soon, I began to discover a pattern in their daily movements. In the mornings, they grazed in their favorite places before heading off to new territories. They drank at their favorite creeks that flowed down from the mountains. They traversed the range land on their favorite trails. I learned how to tell how old their tracks were. I found their traces in footprints and dung markings and the hair they'd leave behind on trees while grooming.

Finding the herds was much harder than I had imagined. I thought that my special connection with horses would draw us together. I knew they had reasons to run from me, but didn't they know I was different? Domesticated horses were like putty in my hands. They loved and honored me, as I did them. Why didn't the wild horses love me? Didn't they know I'd been enlightened by my vision quest? The camel from the fairgrounds had come looking for me when he had lost faith in humans. Why didn't these horses come to me?

After a month in the backcountry, the smaller creatures considered me a resident. The jays no longer announced my arrival; the squirrels made peace with me. The wild creatures felt no need for silence when I passed, and the sounds of the forest echoed around me. Why then did the horses refuse to accept me? Maybe because I was trying to make it happen – to find the horses – rather than letting the horses find me. So many times I had told my friends, "Wait until your horse comes to you."

Of course! It wasn't me the horses rejected. It was my behavior. In my attempts to join them, in their eyes, I was stalking them. The jays and squirrels accepted me because, in their eyes, I wasn't stalking them. But something good actually came from my failed attempts. The horses became less afraid due to my inability to catch up with them. They learned my limitations, but they still saw me as a hunter.

So intent was I on the situation I'd created with the wild horses, I wasn't paying attention to where I was going. I absentmindedly wandered into a stand of pinion pines. The afternoon sun was encroaching on the morning's coolness. The dew sizzled away with the advancing heat, snapping me back to attention.

Suddenly I heard a popping sound I had never heard before. I thought it must be my imagination. I walked a bit further, trying to work my way out of the trees. I thought I heard the sound again but was still not sure, then I heard it again. There! This time I was certain it was real. Maybe it was some kind of animal making the noise. I walked out of the trees into the lower brush country. The popping stopped. I returned to the forest so I could hear it again. There! I ran toward the sound. Nothing. Again ... there! I ran toward the sound, but it had already faded away. I heard the sound again and again. I cocked my head to get a fix on the sound but still could not trace it to any source.

I decided to sit very still and listen. The popping sounds surrounded me. I had never heard anything like them before. What could they be? The sounds began coming in such rapid succession, I wanted to laugh. How absurd! How could there be so much noise all around me, when I couldn't even tell where it was coming from? Slowly, it dawned on me that the sounds were filtering down from above, maybe from something in the tree branches.

I gazed up into the silvery green branches. A tiny, translucent, brown, feather-like something caught my attention. It was about the size of the tip of my thumb, paper thin and split like a fairy's wing – floating, spinning, reeling, lofting, zigzagging on its eccentric journey to the earth. The tiny kite settled at my feet in the residual pine needles carpeting the ground. Even as I watched, it

133

seemed to dig itself into the debris.

More popping sounds erupted just above me. Gazing up into the branches, I noticed the sounds seemed to emanate from the vicinity of a particular pinecone. As I watched, the pinecone exploded with a "pop!" The pinecone spewed out all its little pillow-winged, fairy-like kites. I picked one up. It was olive shaped, like a young tadpole, but flat. Looking more closely, I saw the paper tadpole held a pinion nut. I cracked its envelope and ate the nut. It tasted just like the ones from the grocery store at home.

I peered through the tree's branches out to the valley below. Sky, space and atmosphere were filled with the dance of the next generation of pinion pines. The popping sounds that signaled their birth made staccato music in the air; the wind's shifting currents set their choreography in the sky. Like autumn leaves or apple blossoms, the pinion seed pods danced through the forest on the summer air. Actually, they were the sailing ships of evolution.

I began dancing, celebrating with the trees. I caught the little envelopes that chose to land on my open palm. Gathering them to me, I suddenly had the answer. I now knew how to stop the horses from running. I didn't need to scour the hills, hoping to run across them. If I stayed in one place, as I had done to discover the secret of the popping pines, the horses were bound to run across me. Again, as with my vision quest, nature had provided the solution and path I needed to take.

I set out at once to look for the right spot, starting with the creeks. There were several in the reserve. Some were remote and overgrown with brush, rocks and trees – not as safe for horses as the ones running through the open fields.

Finally I found their main water source, a perennial stream running through a meadow where the horses liked to graze. Over the years, the horses had beaten a path through the stream, worn down its banks, and carved out a bowl-shaped waterhole. From the waterhole, I could see all around for several miles. I chose a knoll overlooking several approaches the horses might use to reach the water and sat down to wait.

After several hours, they suddenly appeared – in clusters, exactly as they had the day of Mustang's return when the herd had joined us in the field. First five horses, then another group, then more horses came into view around the bend. As they stepped into the meadow they began to graze.

In a few moments there were at least forty wild horses and their offspring all around me. These were true mustangs, like my own Mustang, nothing like the domestic varieties the townspeople rode in Indio. Some had Roman noses; others had beautiful chiseled heads like Mustang. They displayed a dazzling mix of color: appys, pintos, bays, blacks, whites, roans, chestnuts, palominos, duns and grays. With such a gaudy array, the herd had mastered the art of invisibility to survive. Rather than blending into their environment like a chameleon, they knew where to be and where not to be. They had perfected their ability to hide, and their ability to escape.

I sat, adrift in a sea of wild mustangs, the cleverest and wildest renegades that had ever refused capture. They had won their fight for freedom and been rewarded with these warm, sunny days and cool breezes – and plenty to eat, as evidenced by their filled out bodies and shiny coats.

Waiting for them to join me had worked but making friends with them was another matter. The horses were aware of me on the hill, yet were not afraid of me. No longer a threat, I had become a mere nuisance. From tracking the horses, I knew they enjoyed community and were keenly aware of their surroundings. I knew they would stay in the same vicinity as long as food was plentiful and travel to new territory when that range became depleted. Because they grazed over a large rangeland, their hooves were well worn. Their glossy coats showed they did not suffer from the parasite problems of domestic horses. They readily used trails laid down by other animals or made their own, forming large cloverleaf paths centered around their water sources.

Watching the herd was like watching a giant, multi-colored mobile. No horse made a movement without it affecting the movement of the group as a whole. The whole herd grazed, tails switching, legs stamping away stinging insects. Occasionally heads popped up to listen for unusual sounds, necks shaking off unwanted flies.

I scanned the herd, identifying individuals and picking out the most beautiful. I spotted mares, foals and yearlings – and a bay stallion. I knew at once he was a stallion because of his presence. His aloof manner and his stance gave him the look of a general on guard. I noticed two other stallions, a black and a pinto. Though they looked even more impressive than the bay, I had no doubt

135

the bay stallion was the ultimate herd leader. He didn't move in unison with the rest of the herd, but stood out in the sea of horses like an island.

I had heard how dangerous stallions were, how unpredictable and aggressive their behavior could be. Children and women were warned not to ride stallions, or even pet one. Our neighbor across the street, Helen, was badly bitten by a stallion and had to keep him locked up in a pen. Despite these warnings and Helen's mishap, I, like all children who love horses, dreamed of a stallion that was devoted to me, that would protect me, and that no one else could manage. Although stallions had a bad reputation, I didn't think it was entirely deserved. I believed everyone had a good side and bad side – even stallions. I believed they could be caring, kind and gentle. I had this relationship with Mustang who retained the instincts and spirit of a stallion, even though he was a gelding.

I had never actually seen a wild stallion before today. Now I would be seeing stallions everyday, real wild stallions!

Wild horses look different than their domesticated cousins; their aliveness and keen awareness sets them apart. Among a wild herd, stallions have thicker necks, fatter jaws, wider muzzles and sleeker coats than the other horses. Their muscle tone and physique is remarkable.

I picked the bay stallion out of the herd as my favorite. I was partial to bays because of Mustang, but this stallion was so special he would have been my favorite no matter what color he was. He was older than the other two. His mane and tail were thick and long and shiny black. He had no markings. His neck was long and arched and he held his head at attention. His coat showed signs of age with some graying around the muzzle and flanks. His stride and cadence were agile for his age even though his hooves were cracked and worn.

He was aware of me the moment my eyes fixed on him. As he looked across the meadow at me, I felt a strong connection. With deep eyes like Strawberry, he was a leader of leaders, like Mustang. I longed to make friends with him, so I brought him closer to me by naming him Mustano.

I spoke his name and it rang in the air like a single word poem, "Mustano."

The bay stallion raised his head high in agreement.

I had named my first wild horse. I felt like a naturalist identifying a new species and labeling it for posterity – only what I had discovered was the world of wild horses.

Since I sought the wisdom of a wild herd leader, I would have to interact with the horses without domesticating their spirit. Already, on my first encounter, I felt accepted into their world because they had not fled from me and because Mustano had heard me call his name.

I believed that what I could learn from these horses would come from their need for companionship. They seemed connected to each other by order and unity and their unquestionable desire to stay together. I felt sure the secret of joining them and being accepted would come from their herd behavior.

I would make a pact with the wild horses. I would agree to their order and unity and their desire for companionship. I would join them on their terms, not on my own.

It had taken a great effort on my part to get close to the herd. I could not get over the fact that I was looking at a herd of horses that had learned to flee from humans and had done so time and time again to win their freedom. Today they honored me with their presence. I could learn all I needed about horse behavior by watching their daily interactions. I rose from the hillside and called to Mustano. He looked up sharply.

"I'll see you tomorrow," I said.

I had no idea if that were true, but I would hold onto that thought until the next encounter.

Carolyn Resnick

Chapter XIX

Dancing With Mustano

Body Language

Hear the voice
Of the Bard!
Who Present, Past and Future sees;
Whose ears have heard the Whole Word
That walked among the ancient trees.
William Blake

Mustano stepped into the meadow, looking for adventure. He trotted around the edge of the field, glancing left and right, checking behind bushes, carrying his tail high like a peacock to show himself off. He was alone, Don Quixote seeking his fortune.

It was early summer. A pair of geese honked their way across a cloudless, blue sky. The edge of the morning light was chasing away the night shadows. I was there, sitting on my favorite perch overlooking the meadow. I couldn't imagine what Mustano was looking for so intently.

To my surprise, Mustano, on his quest for adventure, discovered a roadrunner. The roadrunner is a desert bird that can run almost as fast as a horse. The roadrunner was standing on a rock quite conspicuously, as I had seen his kind do many times before.

I had a perfect view of the encounter and neither Mustano nor the bird knew I was there. Mustano stopped and arched his neck, then did a strange thing, out of character. As I watched in amazement, he leaped at the bird like a cat. The roadrunner sprang into the air, flopped about in the sky, then zinged itself to the ground faster than it had left it. Assuming the posture of a stick, it disguised itself from Mustano.

Mustano seemed pleased with himself. He stood for a moment looking around as if the roadrunner had vanished. Although the bird was standing right in front of his nose, Mustano was unable to see it. Then, out of the blue, he snorted like the cry of a mountain lion. His cry shot across the meadow, scaring the roadrunner into action and exposing its whereabouts – which was a great surprise to Mustano.

The roadrunner sprang up into Mustano's face looking for an escape. The stallion bolted off with the roadrunner in hot pursuit. They circled the meadow's edge. As the roadrunner gained on him, Mustano looked over his shoulder, snatching glances between bouncing canter strides. After a few more yards of bird chasing horse, Mustano regained his composure and confidence, and spun around face-to-face with the roadrunner. The roadrunner slammed on his brakes and resumed his twig-like appearance.

Mustano pranced off like a young colt, looking for more adventure. I had just looked into a world that is hidden to most and witnessed an unusual encounter between two wild creatures. No matter how spontaneous their behavior and how odd to see a bird and horse change roles to ambush each other, I got the feeling this wasn't the first time it had happened. I later found out my suspicions were right.

I had discovered that though he was getting up in years, Mustano still had a playful nature. I wanted to dance with Mustano like I danced with Mustang and Strawberry. I wanted to be the roadrunner. If I could engage Mustano in a morning romp, I felt we could become even closer. I had never had a personal interaction with Mustano.

Today might be my perfect opportunity. Mustano was already in a playful mood and as he was away from his herd, he would be more relaxed and less distracted by his responsibilities.

Mustano's morning adventure was taking him around the edge of the meadow. If he stuck to his path, he was bound to discover me. I waited for him, nervous and excited. I knew that this was my opportunity. How should I introduce myself to enable us to share the same interplay he had enjoyed with the bird? If Mustano would play with me as he had with the roadrunner, something great could happen – something that might give me the key I had been looking for to create a bond between myself and all horses, wild or domestic, trained or untrained, captured or free.

Soon Mustano played and grazed his way around toward where

I was waiting. I couldn't jump out in front of him like I did when inviting Mustang to dance with me. Mustano had a mindset to be afraid of humans.

I ran possibilities through my mind and came up with the idea of posing myself like the roadrunner had done. I stood on a rock holding out my arms more like a scarecrow than a stick. I stood waiting for Mustano to find me as he searched the meadow for adventure.

Pretending not to notice him, I practiced different poses, trying to pick the right one. Suddenly, Mustano snorted his discovery of me. Surprised, I turned around to see Mustano high in the air in a full rearing posture. Off balance, I fell to the ground, forgetting to pose. He stood perfectly still. I jumped away from him, backwards, still looking at him, trying to be playful and inviting in my most horse-like way. He bowed his neck and pawed the ground. I bowed my neck, snorted and pawed the ground back at him. He reacted by stepping toward me as a challenge. This scared me and I ran up into the rocks where I had been sitting. He stood snorting and prancing around. Then leaping into the air, he took off running. His tail flagged the message: "I will return." I came down from the rocks and hid on the backside of a pine tree, waiting for his charge.

In a few minutes he returned, prancing and dancing his way back in zigzag fashion, checking the forest edge in all directions looking for me. He was a hundred feet away when I stepped out from behind the tree. I began prancing and dancing, looking around the forest to express my casualness. I zigzagged my way to him. We were a matched pair of bookends in celebration of newfound friendship.

We pranced around each other and visited together for a few strides. Then Mustano took off in one direction and I in another. On his last approach, Mustano walked slowly toward me with a quiet grace. I stepped back to see what his response would be. He stopped and looked softly at me. It was his way of communicating with me. He understood my movements and chose to speak to me by responding with his own movements. For horses, language is always a dance.

It was my idea to dance, and it was his idea to lead the dance. The connection we shared created a unity in our movements. Every move we made and every breath we took belonged to a rhythm we shared together. We were perfectly matched in movement and could have been dancing on a ballroom floor. His movements brought out a dance in me that I did not know I had. Our interaction could rival any dance team for perfect harmony and grace. I felt that I knew him completely.

My instinct had returned to me. When I first came to live with the wild horses, I had no idea how I would ever get close to the lead stallion. Now I was well on my way. Pretending I was a horse and miming my intent was paying off. I didn't know our morning dance would become a tradition, but as it turned out, this dance became a regular part of Mustano's solo morning adventures.

There is an old story about gaining a wild horse's trust by gently blowing in his nostrils. Mustano taught me the meaning of that story and how it works. It doesn't happen the way we think. It happens when the horse blows gently into our face, not when we blow into his. By his action, he commits to the possibility of friendship.

The magic, I learned, was to speak to Mustano when he wanted to listen – when he searched me out, not the other way around. The magic was not my blowing into his nostrils, but him breathing into mine.

Mustano started off into the forest in the direction of the herd. I stood waiting for another invitation to follow. Mustano again stopped and looked back at me. He turned and walked toward me, then turned again and continued into the forest. I followed behind him. He picked up a path that led us to the other horses.

It was midmorning when we entered the meadow. There we found his band and a few other horses. The herd was engaged in mutual grooming and companion grazing. Two young colts stood at the far end of the meadow lazily mixing mutual grooming with mock fighting, drained of most of their early-morning exuberance.

Mustano took one last look at me, saying, "Good-bye, it was fun." He walked into the meadow, disappearing into his own world once again.

That's the way it is in the company of wild horses. They are in control. I would have enjoyed Mustano's close company and played with him all day. I would have liked to touch him, groom him, ride him, but instead, when he said good-bye, I gave him room. Such is the law and etiquette of the community of wild horses.

If I had tried anything else, I would have lost the ground I had gained in our growing relationship. Although Mustano had accepted me and we shared the same language as morning companions, I knew we had a long way to go. If I did not step over the line, the bond we had created would be there tomorrow. I got lost in the herd, biding my time, waiting for a chance opportunity to dance with Mustano again.

Carolyn Resnick

Chapter XX
Sagebrush, Ambassador of the Herd
Finding the Bottom of the Pecking Order

After a couple weeks of observing the herd at close range, I watched Mustano guarding the herd with unceasing vigilance. I came to realize that his behavior had shaped his bearing and was the reason why I picked him out of all the other stallions even though they were more beautiful because of their color and youth. His bearing shone above all the other stallions. I knew it was created from his ability to lead. He broke up battles that occurred between the dominant horses and the horses that were unfairly picked upon. He played with the young stallions and patiently tolerated the foals and yearlings. All horses respected him, whether they were part of his band or not. It was easy for me to see that he was a good father and family man. He never had to prove his leadership because the horses naturally accepted his authority. His leadership shaped the herd into a society that was admirable.

His favorite mare was a mature white mare I later named Moonlight. I was drawn to her for many of the same reasons I was drawn to Mustano. Most horses at home in Indio were bays or chestnuts. Palominos, blacks, pintos and white horses were unusual and, therefore, quite eye appealing. White horses were my favorite.

Moonlight was not only Mustano's favorite, she was the dominant mare in the herd. Every horse made way for her passage. During the day, she often stood aloof, taking over Mustano's guard duty, especially when he was grazing. She helped Mustano keep the peace. I noticed how she cleverly used the herd for her own protection by surrounding herself with horses while she was grazing. This kept her safe from any predator sneaking up on the herd while she was not on guard. Like Mustano, survival was clearly her greatest focus.

The fact that Moonlight and Mustano were cautious of any possible threat to the safety of the herd created a problem for me trying to inject myself into the herd. They were comfortable with my presence from a distance but they would not let me any closer and following them was out of the question. When I would try to follow along, they would pick up speed until they ditched me. They no doubt thought I was stalking them – up to my same old tricks. Once again, I found myself looking for a new solution to the old problem of getting the horses to accept me. While they accepted me when they came into my space, they resisted my attempts to join them in their travels.

One day something happened in the field that brought the horses closer to me. I found a solution to my problem of not being able to insert myself into the herd in a mare that I had named Sagebrush. I had named her Sagebrush because her mane and forelock were always tangled with sagebrush brambles, a result of her habit of grazing on fresh grass growing among the sagebrush. She was a dominant horse and seemed to derive pleasure from driving off other horses that ventured too close to her when she was engrossed in pulling the grass out of these thorny bushes.

At this point in my relationship, when they were in the field grazing and I got too close, the horses would bolt, trot, or amble away. On this particular day, while heading to the creek to have lunch, I saw my opportunity to make a change in their behavior. I thought that maybe Sagebrush would be brave enough to stand her ground if I tried to approach her. If I could get her to stand her ground, maybe I could set a new standard in how the horses chose to deal with me.

I was hoping she might try to run me off if I got too close to her and the herd. I felt that if I could get her to drive me away, the horses would learn that I could be controlled. They would see that I would be respectful of their rights. I knew if I could exhibit my behavior of respect and vulnerability, the herd might trust me enough to let me join with them in a closer connection.

On my way down to the creek, I found Sagebrush occupied in nibbling some tender grass from a thorny bush. I got as close as I could without her spotting me. When she discovered me, I was a mere twenty feet away. I tensed and with my body language I tried to telegraph that she had frightened me. I waited for her to make a move. She picked up on my behavior and responded by laying her ears back and wrinkling her nose in the most unattractive fashion. She hadn't been a pretty sight before and now her expression was as nasty as her unkempt appearance. She charged me like she had the other horses. I took off running!

The whole herd saw my retreat. This was more than I could have hoped for. In that instant, the horses learned that not only was I slow, but I could be challenged. Things were moving fast, faster than I had anticipated. A frustrating situation had now turned around in only a few weeks. Horses were no longer running away from me. Now they were running toward me – at least, Sagebrush was!

When Sagebrush decided I'd run far enough, and not wanting to get too far away from her bush for fear that another horse might take advantage of her departure, she returned to her bush and continued nibbling.

While Sagebrush was still focused on thorny bushes, I began scouting the field, searching for other thorny bushes. When I found one, I stood guard by it as if I, too, desired the tall grass that grew inside. If my search brought me too close to the other horses in the field, they would now glare at me and I would then quickly move away from them.

In a few days, all the horses were exercising their right to drive me away. They were no longer afraid of me. I understood their laws and I obeyed their wishes. I was, as far as I was concerned, part of their family. However, every horse in the herd disliked me except Mustano, Moonlight and Sagebrush. Mustano and Moonlight ignored me altogether, and, believe it or not, Sagebrush had grown to like me.

Sagebrush discovered that I had a useful purpose and began keeping an eye on me. When she saw me standing still beside a bush, she knew I had found another of her favorite treats. She would trot over, showing pleasure with a twinkle in her eye and her ears perked in anticipation. Anybody happening by would have thought Sagebrush and I had a magical bond like Tarzan with the elephants. If I called Sagebrush, she trotted to me every single time. It wasn't that I'd found a way to train wild horses. What I'd found was more valuable. I'd found the beginnings of acceptance.

Wild horses keep their distance from humans because of how they perceive us. Unlike dogs, cats, and other domesticated animals, wild horses naturally fear humans. They fear us because we behave rudely toward them. Not that we know we are being rude, we simply don't understand the signals horses give us for keeping our distance. We often invade their right to be left alone and we don't understand their rules of passage. They are also instinctively suspicious of anyone who isn't a herd member.

As I respected their space and freedom and spent most of the day with them, they started adopting me into their ways. I had moved up the ladder. I had graduated from nuisance to mascot. Now when Moonlight and Mustano left the field, I could travel with the herd on their journeys. The horses no longer ran to ditch me because they knew I was under control. More and more, I realized that it was only a matter of time that the horses would come to trust me completely.

I knew that traveling with a herd of wild horses would teach me their ways. I would see the world with wild horses as my tour guides. Being accepted as part of the herd, even though it was from the bottom of the pecking order, I was attending their school, learning their laws, their pecking order, their love of community, their body language.

What Sagebrush offered me was a gateway to the world of horses. Over the years, I discovered every herd has a Sagebrush. What I mean by this is that every herd has at least one horse who will defend her rights. If you look around, you'll find her, with a smirk on her face and a dirty nose, looking for trouble – the ambassador of the herd.

Sagebrush exhibited continual pecking order behavior. Without her, I would have had to wait long intervals between a horse enforcing or requesting behavior from another horse. Without her, observing horse communication and interaction would have been like waiting for shooting stars or Haley's Comet. But thanks to Sagebrush, I was getting an accelerated education, like a lesson taught using time-lapse photography as a teaching aid.

When I started watching the herd for signs of communication, at first I could only see major skirmishes that occurred once in a while. Later on, I started noticing subtleties in the horses' interaction. The more I learned about the rules, the do's and don'ts of pasture law and the ranking of each horse, I began to notice interactions and communication that were taking place all the time right under my nose.

Sagebrush, too, benefited from our relationship. She had an extra scout helping her search for sweet, grassy thorn bushes. Soon she became attached to me and would hang out with me just for my companionship. She got jealous of other horses that came too close to me. When I lay down in the field, she stood over me taking naps in the afternoons.

Sagebrush and I started out on a bad note, but now, I really was her best friend. In only a few days, Sagebrush became a wild horse desiring my companionship. She preferred me over all the other horses. Even if her reason for liking me was not based on the purest motive of friendship, we were becoming closer everyday. This gave me hope that other hoses would come to a closer relationship with me as well.

As time went on, I became aware that communication between the horses was not an occasional or sporadic occurrence. My view changed. Now I could compare them to chatterboxes in a noisy restaurant.

Eventually the horses reminded me of the Mad Hatter's Tea Party. Like at the tea party, it was almost always four o'clock in the field of horses. Like at the Mad Hatter's Tea Party, they had to have order, a little conversation, a little something to eat and most of all, a desire to listen and be heard. This desire to listen and be heard is when the trouble began. While the tea party in *Alice in Wonderland* seemed orderly and harmonious at first glance, Alice soon discovered great tension and chaos beneath the surface. Likewise, while I saw the horses as orderly and harmonious, beneath the surface I soon discovered constant dynamics of communication between horses. Ear flicks and tail swishes were part of a communication system. One horse even slightly shifting position conveyed an important message to nearby horses. I learned that harmony among horses is maintained by a constant undercurrent of communication and herd interaction. I eventually saw that for the herd to be in the most harmonious state, communication between the horses must be at its peak.

When harmony is flowing through the herd, every horse is at the right place at the right time. This harmony is accomplished through pecking order. The main purpose of pecking order is to maintain unity. Horses in unity are like a large drill team, only more effective. They seem to find their place and work in step as if by a magnetic connection, much like the connection that geese have in the unity of flight.

I saw parallels between creatures as diverse as geese and horses, each having a common language and purpose within their flocks and herds. A closer look into nature showed me that animals have amazing skills that are hard for us to understand. A bird building a nest with just its beak seems impossible to me. After watching birds building their nests, I still feel I am missing the key element in how they build it and how it holds together. With all my tools, fingers, reasoning and observation, I still cannot build a nest.

The subtlety of interaction that binds horses together in a herd was as difficult to see and comprehend as understanding how a bird creates a strong nest from a pile of twigs. The unspoken thread in the relationship that unites the herd might be compared to the innate knowledge birds use to engineer their nests. It is an innate knowledge they are born with.

I saw horses like a moving nest. Though I never understood the ingredient that holds a nest together, I came to understand what holds the herd together. I learned how to use their connection to assimilate into the herd. I was able to join with them in their moving nest. I was a twig in the fiber of their unity. It came to me through observation.

After looking back over the past few months, I examined all that I had learned. That summer I learned to use patterns in the topography to navigate. I learned to use my instincts to find my way home. I learned how to keep the herd from running. I learned how to gain the wild horses' acceptance enough to join them in their travels.

It was my relationship with Sagebrush that opened the next door. I was looking for acceptance at the bottom of the pecking order, which I knew would build trust throughout the community. I don't think there was any other way to be assimilated into Mustano's band except by starting at the bottom of the pecking order and working my way up because of the extreme fear these horses had of my presence. By watching and observing the herd, I learned many secrets that I could never learn from books.

My experiences with Sagebrush on grazing rights and Mustano's dance were the building blocks of my Liberty Training, Beyond the Whisper™ program I use today. I hope that sharing my experience with you will shed some light on how horses respond and how interacting with them can shape their behavior.

Mustano was looking to dance with me when I danced with him. I made friends with Sagebrush when she needed to protect her territory from me. From there I was able to get her to accept a relationship with me by allowing her to be dominant over me. Most often, giving dominance to a horse is not a good thing, but sometimes it is very helpful in building trust when fear is in the way. From giving her a belief in her power and helping her find thorn bushes, we developed a relationship that turned into a friendship we shared together.

Harmony and teamwork is how horses are able to survive the elements, and when we put our focus on building these skills with horses, we can connect into a one-mind consciousness in unity of shared movements like the ones found in nature. We can see this connection in schools of fish, migrating birds, stampeding horses or the harmony of a foal shadowing its mother in flight. While it is beautiful to watch, it is more powerful to experience.

Chapter XXI
White Horses in the Moonlight
How Moonlight Got Her Name

Why is it that some people can use a small gesture and get a favorable response from a horse, while others make the same gesture and get no response at all? It comes from a strong bond shared between horse and human, and from an innate ability to emote the kind of feeling that will influence a horse's behavior in a positive way. The naivety of a child lends great insight into how to connect with horses. Our childhood memories can return us to the indelible connection of the heart.

A horse can recognize a horse lover. People who are full of joy, or strongly sad, or who have a spiritual connection to nature are like magnets to horses. The more heart you have for life, the stronger the connection you can share. Horses are mostly spirit driven and are drawn to people who are drawn to them.

As a child I had an extreme need to connect with white horses because they were my favorite color. Throughout history white horses have been depicted in myths to possess supernatural powers. From the perspective of a child, I believed that there was some truth in these myths, and it led me to understand that deep feelings of the heart can be trusted.

This story is to point out the value of finding a feeling place in working with horses and to honor Moonlight with a tribute—indeed the naming of Moonlight led me to the discovery that the myth of the power of white horses is based in truth.

The white mare came toward me moving softly through the damp morning grass. Above her the waning moon shone translucent in the brightening air. Her name came to me then, as I knew it would, without thought or effort. Moonlight.

Mustano, Sagebrush and Moonlight. Each wild horse's name popped into my head freely as our friendships formed. Each name came with a story. Instinctively, I named the white mare Moonlight, without understanding until much later the power of her name and its significance.

When I was a child, the moon and I were best friends. I spent time with her so she would glow. I felt she glowed because she was loved. She glowed because of the coyotes' howl, because of lovers in the moonlight. She glowed for everyone that cared. The moon was my special friend.

My mother showed me how to catch the moon's reflection in a bucket and how to make it jump from one bucket to another. In the evenings we took turns singing songs that had the word moon in them. My favorites were "It's Only a Paper Moon," "Shine On, Harvest Moon," "Blue Moon," and "Moonlight and Roses." My mother's favorite song went like this:

Me and the moon,
We'll be keeping company.

I ask the moon to tell me
Where under the stars you are.
I ask the moon to tell you
How dear to me you are.

'Cause me and the moon,
We'll be keeping company.

When I was old enough, I rode Mustang out to the white sands and read out loud to the light of the moon. I listened to the night pass and to howling coyotes, crickets and locusts. I watched Mustang listen to the night. I sat in his shadow and looked up at his back lit coat silhouetted against the night sky and watched his four white socks dancing alone in the moonlight.

Many cultures believe there is something about white horses that makes them different from all other horses. They believe white horses possess great power. I believed it too. The first time I saw a white horse in the moonlight, I felt the moment was reaching out to share the secret of this myth with me.

The moon in the desert lights up the night. Like the sun, she casts deep shadows and is bright enough for reading a book. The moon seeks out and spotlights white objects: desert sand, white roses and the tails of cotton tail rabbits. There would be no chance to hide in the moonlight for an animal with a white coat. White horses stand out like no others; they appear like powerful, magnificent spirits in moonlight while all other horses simply go unnoticed.

White horses cannot hide, and from this I learned that white horses sleep in the dark of the moon and need to stay on guard in the moonlight while others rest. They have no camouflage and rest little. The ones that survive from predators are stronger, braver and wiser than the horses that surround them

White horses are the record keepers of hard times, like Crazy Horse. They stand in harmony with their surroundings, prepared, knowing that ahead could lie tragedy. Intruders are the enemy, and white horses wait and watch for them to appear on the horizon. Deep feeling of the heart for all things increases horsemanship skills by the kinship it fosters. I designed the cover of my book to express the connection I shared with Moonlight that led to the writing of *Naked Liberty*.

Moonlight began my interest in mythology and how it can bring deeper meaning to life experience. I learned from her how to use a spiritual connection in horse training. Moonlight would have held a lot of ill will if I had tried to train her without a bond. Staying connected to the memories of childhood makes each experience I have with a horse unique, by treating every training situation with the respect I gave her.

Moonlight rides on white horses,
like a beacon in the night.
In the white horses' dance
they see and predict
their own outcome
for another day unharmed.

Chapter XXII

A Foal's First Lessons

How Horses Train Horses

Fully unfolded, half dry and more than ready to meet the challenge of his new life, the urge to stand took hold of him. Like a butterfly bursting from a cocoon, he stood on all fours, trembling from the effort it took to hold himself up. When he tried to take a step, he went down like a crab running sideways, collapsing and crashing to the ground. Giving the fall due consideration, he lay for few moments panting with his head held high and his legs tucked under him. The struggle to survive begins at birth and so do the lessons.

Though his mother was Moonlight, she had foaled in the dark of the moon. Instinct guided her to a safe place at the meadow's edge away from the herd. Here Moonlight had given birth and here she would stay with her newborn until the bond was set. After her labor, Moonlight was red-tailed and pink-bottomed, but her colt was black as the just-fled night, save for an unusual white marking above his eyes like a white thumbprint in the middle of his forehead. His tail was already twisting furiously, covered with kinky, short, damp hair. I named him "Blackstone."

Minutes ago he'd been inside his mother, held tight in the birth canal. Suddenly he was pushed into another world and his skin came alive to the touch of the wind and his mother's tongue. Now he had room to move – and room to fall. It was a lot to consider. I knew he was deep in concentration. His conscious mind was having a long conversation with his instincts.

He lay motionless and then, with no warning, he flew up from the ground like a rocket. He took his first walking steps, then broke into a full run, halting after a short distance. He paused to consider the consequences of his actions; there were none. So he took off again, his running spurts growing longer and longer.

As suddenly as his desire to stand came the instinct to nurse. His sucking lips were an audible, visual sign that settled his mother. She waited patiently for him to find her teat, guiding him with nudges to show him the way to the colostrum, an essential for his survival. After nursing a while, Blackstone found new strength. His second wind propelled him once more across the meadow. His mother darted after him, murmuring low, trying to get her foal's attention.

It was quite a task. Moonlight and Blackstone had not yet bonded. The foal was having an adventure, and at top speed – without fears and without cares. His ego swelled with pride and he displayed his joy in his newfound freedom. He reached out with his long legs to greet this new world. He soon learned that if he did not look down he would not fall. Like all foals, he was a quick learner, and his proud carriage was a sign that he showed promise of being a lead stallion like his father Mustano.

Then suddenly Blackstone discovered me and, without warning, bolted toward me. Moonlight knew this was not a good thing and tried to get between us, but Blackstone was not to be deterred. I tried to help by moving away, but every time I turned to leave, Blackstone followed me. Then I remembered horses' natural response to objects moving around them. They instinctively shy from anything approaching and gravitate toward anything moving away. So I turned on Blackstone and headed straight for him. Taking advantage of the opportunity I created, Moonlight wheeled and raced off in the opposite direction.

Seeing me advancing and his mother departing, his instincts took over. He screamed in alarm and raced to her side. Moonlight circled the field, running and prancing with her tail flagged. Her trumpeting echoed across the valley. Blackstone glued himself to her side. When Moonlight stopped in the distance and settled down to graze, Blackstone began nursing. The bond was set.

Blackstone took longer than most foals to develop this bond. Son of Mustano and Moonlight – herd leaders of a collection of the strongest, fastest renegades in the valley – Blackstone was born with courage.

In these first minutes of life, the dark-moon colt was learning a lifetime of lessons, as all free creatures do. From now on, Blackstone would expect and be prepared for the unforeseen, for a life of discovery and decision-making. These early experiences were imprinting him with a profound, yet basic survival skill, the art of blending instinct with judgement.

I was learning, too. Blackstone's first lesson in bonding taught me that foals are equipped at birth to respond to movement. They follow anything leaving and move away from anything advancing. Under natural conditions, this innate response to movement stays with a horse throughout his life. It keeps the herd together and is instrumental in managing and maintaining the pecking order. The herd's entire chain of command relies on the horses' ability to influence each other. It is a process of horses training horses through their instinctive response to movement. A dominant horse is one that understands how to influence another horse with movement and body language. The horse with the most ability to influence the movement of the entire herd is the leader. In a stampede, a lead horse can turn chaos into order, creating a percussion of hooves as unified as a drum roll.

Blackstone and Moonlight were the beginning of this understanding and gave me a day I will never forget.

Blackstone's beginnings started my fascination for what I can learn from newborn foals. Blackstone grew to be a leader of leaders like his father. It was important to see how he experienced his lessons and how he developed his character from what he learned. My relationship with horses has turned out to be one big scientific experiment in the ways of natural development.

I have borrowed the skills of a lead horse to use in my own relationship with horses. Communicating with horses as lead horses do is an invaluable tool. Not only can I move a horse away from me, I can draw a horse to me by leaving him. Between these two responses, horses are easily managed if the bond has been established.

The language of horses is movement. Communicating through a horse's instinctive response to movement creates a well-adjusted horse. Using this language of movement in training not only bonds the horse to me but also develops a magical relationship. The performance we share together is a reflection of our partnership and friendship in unity.

I am drawn to wild horses that rank high in the pecking order. They are easier to train because they pay more attention to body language than other horses, they have more ability to stay focused, they have a great need for companionship and they understand the importance of teamwork. All horses have a desire to follow a leader and when I ask a lead horse to perform a task for me, he is quick to understand what I am asking him to do. He is naturally more cooperative and his willingness to perform for me is immediate.

From my findings over the years, I concluded that the first two weeks of a foal's life with his mother are the most important. It is during this time that his potential for future training and his ability to perform in the show ring are developed. The bonding experience makes for a well-adjusted foal with vigor and an emotional well-being that creates in him a need for companionship. This need for his mother's companionship is essential if the horse is later to have the capacity to bond with humans.

When the foal has completed his initial lessons with his mother, I start my relationship with him. By repeating the lessons he learned from his mother, I reinforce these lessons of social behavior and communication. Through learning these social skills, horses develop their own language. Their skills are developed through pecking order. This is why understanding pecking order is very beneficial in training horses. Watching Blackstone's early development showed me how I could use pecking order to my advantage.

Nursing is a foal's first lesson in communication. Unlike humans, the foal must problem-solve and develop social skills with his mother to be able to nurse. He can't always nurse when he wants to; he must learn manners and accept his mother's direction.

His second lesson is realizing his responsibility to keep up with his mother. After months of following her around and dealing with her moods, he learns how to fit in and keep up. Once this behavior pattern is set, he must learn another important lesson that he instigates himself. As he matures, he will begin adventuring out on short trips without his mother. When he returns, his behavior will be more aggressive and he will turn around and give her a swift kick. When the mother has had enough of this behavior and the foal is old enough to both understand discipline and to display inappropriate intent in aggression, she will reprimand him with a warning kick herself. By doing this, the mother teaches him that all horses have a right to, and indeed will demand, a personal space. It also teaches that there are consequences to his behavior.

The newborn foal's innate response to movement, the lessons his mother teaches and his desire for companionship are the keys to his trainability.

When I begin my training, I am careful not to erase any of the behaviors instilled by the mother. I do this by allowing the foal to choose to interact with me, rather than me introducing the lessons to him through forced interaction. When I set a bond with a foal, the connection he shares with me becomes stronger than the connection he shares with other horses because I focus my lessons with him on bonding games he enjoys playing. I have found that by letting a foal be in charge of his relationship with me, he finds learning fascinating.

I owe a large part of my success in raising foals to what I learned watching foals being born and raised by their mothers in the wild. How the mother presented lessons to her foal, the order in which she presented them and how the foal responded to her lessons are the keys to my approach to horse training.

Had I tried to understand the dynamics between a mother and her foal before I understood the dynamics of a herd, the mother's interaction with her foal would have meant little to me. The knowledge of horse communication I learned through observing herd behavior gave me the ability to distinguish between what the foal instinctively knew at birth and what he was learning. I could tell when his mother was instructing him. I could understand how he was learning his lessons. I was able to piece together the when, what and how that the mother was communicating to her foal by using what I had learned watching a herd interact in the wild.

Blackstone's birth impressed upon me how quickly a foal's life unfolds and how important the initial relationships in life are to the learning process. Over the years, I have made every effort to witness as many births as I could in order to study the development of the foal's learning process. From each, I have gained valuable information to use in training horses. It seems to me that the first step to a horse's acceptance is best gained from the natural process of how a foal learns his first lessons from his mother and how he learns the rules for communication. This is where it begins for every horse. This beginning is the link that binds the herd into a working society; it is how horses train horses. Observing early development in foals is beneficial to everyone who wants to develop their skills with horses. Once equipped with an understanding of herd behavior, observing the early development of foals sheds light on how to bond with and train horses.

Chapter XXIII

Leader of Leaders

The Magical Map

In their everyday need for survival, horses have created a communication system that is noteworthy. Wild horses are like a society of nomadic people who have leaders of leaders. Because nature's habitat for horses is open rangeland, each horse has freedom to pick and choose a band of horses where he or she fits in and where his or her personality type is needed. Fights are usually between consenting scrappers, while the submissive are protected by onlookers. From the herd instinct of horses, core values and laws are developed that support the needs of the whole community, from the strongest to the weakest individual.

Spring was nearly over and my second summer with the wild horses was at my doorstep. I reviewed my three-year plan. The first summer, my goal was simply to observe the wild horses. Through much legwork, I had achieved my goal and learned a great deal about horse behavior. I had danced with Mustano, watched Moonlight and her foal and developed a friendship with Sagebrush.

This summer my goal was to become part of Mustano's band and be able to take orders and give orders from the group, lead mare and stallion. This was a lot to expect, but I had learned so much about horse behavior and I felt this knowledge would help me assimilate into the herd.

When the day finally arrived, I found everything as I had left it the summer before except for some new stock pens and fencing down on the lower meadow close to the highway that ran along the short side of the reserve. I figured the new fence was to keep the next group of horses brought in for movie work from escaping into the back hills like the herd I was studying had done years before.

The land was much drier this year and the horses had formed smaller groups than the big herd I had found them in last summer. The bachelor colts had been driven out of the family unit or had banded together on their own. Sultan, the black stallion, Cochise, the paint stallion, and Mustano separated from each other and were keeping their mares away from all other horses in the search for greener pastures. Sultan and Mustano were hard at work trying to separate their mares so they could continue on their own ways. The bickering mares were making a lot of trouble for the two stallions – so much trouble that my arrival went virtually unnoticed.

Since I knew the land well, it took me no time to run across Mustano's band. When I found them, his mares were entangled with Sultan's mares. Both bands had come to the watering hole at the same time of day, a habit developed when the grazing lands were rich. At that time, all the horses had run together as one big herd.

Mustano had two problems: first, not to insult the black stallion's mares by moving too aggressively toward them and, second, to reprimand his own mares and separate them from Sultan's herd. He nickered at the mares that were out of his reach and talked to the mares close at hand by lowering his neck and rolling his head in the direction he wanted the mares to take. He rushed at a few to threaten a bite or kick while always keeping an eye on Sultan.

Sultan was a mustang that looked like an Andalusian. Mustano and Sultan were about the same size, fifteen hands. Both were well-bodied horses, but Sultan was in his prime. His shiny, black coat reflected the surrounding chaparral like a mirror. He moved like a crystalline shadow. His conformation was well proportioned, long and low in the tail set. He had a slight Roman nose and large eyes, well placed, set wide enough to give him an attractive look. Still, my heart belonged to aging Mustano because of his courage, strength and leadership. Had these two stallions battled that day, I knew Mustano would have won.

Mustano and Sultan finally cut their mares from each other's band and continued their separate ways. I could see that this sort of incident was going to happen often this summer, which would make for very interesting study.

Mustano's band comprised two bay mares, one dun, two roan chestnut mares and of course, Moonlight. Both roans had foals at their sides. The dun, Sagebrush, was pregnant, due any moment.

One bay mare had a foal; the other showed no sign of any offspring. Moonlight was in excellent health. Blackstone was at her side, growing big and strong. A year older, his coat was now gray. I could see he was going to be white like his mother. Until the waterhole incident, there had been three two year olds, a filly and two colts. I could not tell who their mothers were as they hung around each other, no longer interacting with their mothers.

I realized what a job it must be for Mustano to keep his band together. Already, he had lost the three two-year olds while gathering his mares in the episode at the water hole. Sultan had inadvertently scared the three youngsters and they'd raced up the embankment and disappeared into the brush. Now Mustano had eleven horses.

Had the youngsters not split from the herd, it may have been only a matter of time before Mustano or one of the older mares would have driven them away. They had reached an age where they could threaten the older mares' breeding program. The mustangs' breeding season begins as the weather turns warm in the spring and early summer. At that time, the mares become jealous of the stallions' attention. Lead stallions tend to be more attracted to their older mares while ignoring the younger ones. The pecking order among the mares is largely determined by hormonal richness and physical well being. Favor with the lead stallion moves a mare up in the pecking order.

Driving away the two-year-olds is nature's way of preventing inbreeding. Bachelor herds are a collection of young stock that choose to leave their bands, or are driven out by a mare or stallion, or by the community as a whole. The bachelor horses find each other and form temporary herds of their own. These bachelor herds lack a true leader, even though a young stallion or mare will rise to the head of the pecking order.

After watching the horses for several weeks, I learned the mare's rankings. After Moonlight came Sagebrush. The two bays were in third and fourth positions, with the roan mares at the bottom. The young had their own pecking order, though generally, the older ones were dominant over the younger.

At birth, a lead mare's foal usually holds high rank with his peers and community. The foal of a mother with low status usually holds low rank. As horses intermingle, lower ranking horses can temporarily dominate higher ranking horses, but only if the higher ranking horse is in the mood to exhibit submission. It's like the game, "King of the Hill." Horses can make short-term alterations in their status by their positions on the land relative to each other. Lead horses know this and use it to their advantage.

The Push From Behind

Though it may seem odd, a horse that is walking behind another horse is in the dominant position. If the horse behind is lower in the pecking order, he may not know how to take advantage of this position to dominate. I always wondered why the horse behind holds the dominant position since that position puts the horse in jeopardy; a kick could easily injure the trailing horse. This behavior may have evolved from predators approaching from the rear.

No matter how odd it appears to me that a position of power could come from being behind, I owe my success as a horse communicator to this discovery. From watching lead horses capitalize on this position of power and horses of lower ranks pushing horses of higher rank when they were in this position, I discovered I could use it myself as a communication aid.

I feel my success with horses has grown as my understanding has grown of what drives a horse. My ability to use the dominant position from behind to help develop a working relationship and get rid of bad behavior in horses is a key element in my training. The result of pushing a horse forward like a lead horse encourages the horse to "stick to me" like he would to a band of horses. More importantly, it has the amazing impact in our relationship of creating a deep affection between us.

The first time I experimented with using the dominant position, the bond it produced surprised me as much as when I learned that a horse behind another horse held the dominant position. Communicating from this dominant position, I created a unity between the horse and me that I could feel in my bones. At the moment the horse understood I had asked him to join me like a lead horse, I could feel an energy greater than my own that we were sharing. I felt I had plugged into the horse's spirit. The connection we shared is similar to the connection horses share when they are celebrating a run together – simply enjoying movements in unity.

A notion of the complexity of herd behavior and the reasoning behind a horse holding a dominant position behind another horse is best explained through the dictionary's definition of the words herd and herd instinct. From the definitions, I found an explanation hidden in the meaning of our own language.

The dictionary has two meanings for the word herd. Herd can be a noun or a verb. Herd, as a noun, is "a number of animals feeding or staying together." Herd, as a verb, means "to gather or stay or drive as a group." Even the noun form points out the action of "staying together," a behavior necessary for the noun to exist. Without this action, the meaning of the word is lost.

Looking at the verb form, "to …drive as a group," the best way to drive something forward is to push it from behind. Because horses are flight animals, they can easily be pushed, making this the reason for the dominant position behind, when accompanied by pursuit from behind.

The next part of this dynamic is the definition of the word herd instinct: "… the instinct to think and believe like the majority." All horses in the wild, no matter what their rank or personality type, work to stay together, creating a common herd mentality. Thus, from this herd mentality comes an agreement that they will stay together and follow a leader for their mutual good. As explained earlier, they also give way to each other from the dominant push from behind. It is a push/pull dynamic that causes even the lead horse to surrender to a horse that is behind him, if he feels the push.

From watching lead horses, I found that they are crucially aware of the instinctual effect this push has on other horses. Lead horses use this instinct to direct the horses around them rather than forcing supremacy through pecking order disputes. By comparison, a dominant horse's understanding of the instinctual response to the push is crude, but from that crudeness springs a complete order brought about by the battles the dominant horses engage in.

In the overall picture, this position of being behind has another purpose besides dominance. It serves a practical purpose for herds traveling overland together. The best working example is a stampede. Front runners in a stampede need to keep ahead of the horses behind them. If dominant horses were in front, they might slow the herd down if they did not agree that the horses behind them have the right-of-way.

I have heard and read several accounts of American Indians

walking after a wild horse until the horse turned around and faced them; from their pursuit, they could gain control and the trust of a wild horse.

I learned the importance of this dominant position from watching new arrivals in an established herd being moved around by a dominant member of the herd for an extended time before being accepted into the herd with rank and status. When I tried it myself, I found it so beneficial that it has become one of the rituals I use in my Liberty Training, Beyond the Whisper™ method.

From experimenting, I also found that I must be careful that the horse does not perceive me as a predator when I am moving him forward. He must perceive that I am moving him from the territory he is on rather than pursuing him. He must feel that he is being pushed away rather than chased. It is subtle, but it is the key to achieving a lasting bond.

I found that round pens are too confining. The horse must be able to escape all influence, if he wants to, by running off and declaring another territory. When he has found his new spot and is at complete peace with the idea that he has the power to escape my influence, I slowly walk into his new territory and push him forward again. In a short time, the horse responds to his instincts and the social rules he has learned from other horses and from his mother.

I am requesting from him that he accept my leadership and friendship. From my quiet pursuit, he begins to listen to his instinct that is above all other, that is, his desire to follow a leader. A horse is a herd animal and feels safe and protected in the herd. At that moment, he understands my wishes; at that same moment, I have made an important connection with his spirit.

From my studies of horses in the wild and their acceptance of me, I learned there is no better way to communicate than with their own system of language and laws. Learning how to use their language and laws nurtures my soul and well-being. Speaking to them in their silent language gives me a heightened awareness that binds us together as family and into their world of nature. I believe that this information of horses' social behavior is as beneficial to others as it is to me.

Horses live in a complicated society that cannot be measured simply by instinctual response; however, much of their rich culture most definitely springs from two instinctual reactions: staying together as a herd and yielding to the push/pull response.

Because of their need for each other and their constant daily interactions, horses have a heightened awareness for who really cares for them and who really doesn't. They judge humans by where we put our focus, how we serve their needs, and how we treat them. If we pass their test, we produce a horse with an extraordinary spirit that he is willing to share. They then also give willingly of their horsepower that we seek.

The Code: Rules Set by the Herd That the Lead Horse Honors

It amazed me to look back on what I had learned about the community of wild horses. My observations from the first summer taught me that many bands can join together as one large community when pasturelands are at the top of their production. When this happens, one stallion will be the leader of all the bands making up the herd. This stallion will embody more care-taking qualities than the other stallions.

Furthermore, I observed three major behaviors in horses: Leadership behavior, dominant behavior and submissive behavior. These behaviors are personality types as well.

Herds are made up of the right balance of personalities, with each personality fitting perfectly in the chain of command. If the herd makeup is not harmonious, horses tend to move on until they find a herd they are more suited for.

An important difference between lead horses and dominant horses is that dominant horses show no interest in leadership issues such as where the herd should go for food or how to escape from danger. Rather, they are interested in dominance issues such as maintaining or raising their position in the pecking order.

Through observing Mustano's daily responsibilities, I learned that dominant stallions had a natural desire to follow his lead because of his ability to handle the needs of the herd at large. For this reason, a lead horse is generally the most intelligent horse in the herd. In general, the higher a horse's rank, the more intelligent he or she is.

Mustano had a great desire to collect, manage and direct a herd. Most lead horses can be rated on their skill in leadership by how many mares they are able to collect and manage. However, this formula did not apply to Mustano; his band of mares was smaller than other stallions. But when the horses came together in the summer, his leadership skill was greater than the stallions with larger bands than his own. He was always the leader in any gathering – the leader of leaders.

It was as though he foresaw his responsibility. He knew that to carry out this leadership position over a large territory, he needed to keep his band of mares small so he could split his time between his own band and the needs of the rest of the herd.

Another reason for Mustano's small band was his close relationship with Moonlight and the natural affection he showed her. Although he was attentive to the rest of his mares, it seemed more like they needed him and he responded out of his obligation to their care.

In the large herd, it was Mustano's job to maintain peace and keep the horses focused and alert for any threat to the herd's safety. While Mustano oversaw the herd community at large, Moonlight kept his mares together. Watching Moonlight and Mustano work together in a herd was like watching a shepherd and his dog work together in a flock of sheep. They were that connected and that effective.

From Mustano's point of view, the purpose of leadership was to keep the herd working together in a unified manner for a common good. His attention to keeping peace and his watchfulness for predators created an ecosystem of safety and a one-mind consciousness of what was truly important for survival. The reason he had so much authority and did not need to be aggressive is that all the horses appreciated the safety and stability he brought to the herd.

Over the years, I have seen that with horses put together in a herd by humans, the lead horse at first acts much like a horse with a submissive personality. The lead horse, whether it is a lead stallion or a lead mare, is simply waiting for the horses to sort out their pecking order. Once the order is established, he or she knows that the horses will naturally be able to accept his or her direction. Lead horses at first will avoid any conflict. I have even seen them run to escape from a dominant horse.

In herd formation, pecking order battles start with a greeting ceremony. Lead horses often keep their distance and refrain from greeting other horses, thus avoiding the inevitable battle. Lead horses seldom get into a battle with a new rival because they will not approach a horse that is not ready to recognize their authority.

In setting up pecking order in the beginning, dominant horses are not looking for submissive horses to push around. Rather, they are looking for other dominant horses to battle and settle the dominance issue. They are not interested in fighting a horse that is clearly submissive.

Another thing I have noticed is that lead horses seem to get along with other lead horses and work out who will lead without much fuss and, in some cases, no fuss at all. Instead of demanding pecking order, they seem more interested in picking order. It is like they naturally agree from the start what order they plan to use.

If two lead horses disagree on their rank in the pecking order, they establish their rank much differently than dominant horses. Whereas dominant horses engage each other in open battle, lead horses will ambush their opponent when he is off guard. There seems to be an unwritten rule that horses must submit to any horse that catches them off guard. In my training, this knowledge works like magic to teach aggressive horses to respect my authority.

By watching other horses respond to Mustano, I soon learned that they were following an unwritten code. It became clear that they knew only how to respond to the code while Mustano knew how to apply the code to win his position of leadership. He had to follow the code of the herd to win their loyalty.

The code looks something like this:
If I pay attention and accept your authority and leadership, you have no right to pick on me.
If you ask me to do something that is for my own good, I am happy to follow your leadership.
If I do not pay attention, I will lose my rank.
If you are a tough guy, we can see who is dominant right now.
If I cannot find a leader to follow, it is my job to lead.

All horses know and respond to these rules. Horses can sense when their behavior is inappropriate from lessons they learned growing up with their mothers and lessons they learned from older horses in the family unit.

The most important rule in the horses' code is to pay attention. One way a horse can gain rank over another horse without a direct battle is to catch his opponent off guard. I often saw Mustano watch for the dominant stallion's lack of focus, then sneak up behind him. Caught off guard, the dominant horse ran off embarrassed. Then, after sniffing the spot, Mustano would proceed to defecate and urinate on the territory he had claimed from the inattentive dominant horse.

Horses do not live gentle lives, even though the natural condition they share together is spent in harmonious herd behavior. Harmony is achieved through leadership that doesn't come easily. Mustano was responsible for keeping the harmony by enforcing fair social behavior with the horses that were too aggressive. He avoided physical conflict by enforcing rules of behavior through aggressive body language at the moment a horse would naturally run in terror. This behavior caused a dominant horse to surrender to the laws of the community rather than his own unfit, dominant behavior. Mustano learned early that dominant horses pick fights while lead horses ambush dominant horses that don't pay attention to the lead horse. This is the law of the plains animals.

Using Horse Instinct in Training at Liberty

Knowing the horses' code of rules is very helpful in training a horse. To establish leadership and gain a horse's respect and cooperation, a trainer does not need to be physically aggressive. Physical strength is not an issue with the horse. Leadership is not a show of force but applying the rules of the herd society. Lead horses seem to present their leadership with magnetic charm that all horses are naturally drawn to and cannot resist. A horse's willingness to follow comes as the leader applies a code of rules that is fair and just and that all horses respect. A good lead horse offers safety and well-being to the herd. Such leadership is not resented.

Because people don't understand pecking order, many feel intimidated when correcting a dominant horse. They worry about the horse getting even. Knowing how horses interact with each other will help them deal with their horse more confidently. Pecking order in horses is not as aggressive as some might imagine. Horses do not have an underlying resentment of authority nor a desire to take over leadership. They naturally understand that leadership behavior should be respected. Lead horses have a natural desire to cooperate and, amazingly, will even take direction from a lower ranking horse if the direction makes sense and is given to them without force. This is valuable information in relating to horses because they respond the same way with humans. Dominant horses also naturally desire to follow a leader without force. However, they also understand that aggressive behavior can always be challenged. Trainers who are too aggressive may cause their horse to believe he has a right to defend himself.

Lead horses do not reprimand negative behavior at the time it occurs. Doing so would lower the horse's status in the eyes of other horses. Rather, the leader waits to communicate his power when an offending horse clearly knows he has broken a rule. Likewise, if a horse breaks the code and becomes too aggressive, I do not respond to that behavior. Rather, I restore the horse's desire to follow my lead and wait to catch him off guard. Then I drive him out of the area in which he lost his focus.

My Liberty Training, Beyond the Whisper™ method consists of handpicked interactions lead horses use with other horses. Using them myself, I have had extraordinary success in both establishing a deep bond with horses and creating a desire in horses to accept my direction. I follow their code of rules, shying away from battles like a lead horse would.

Understanding the basic nature of horses helps people succeed with them. The best way to learn the nature of horses is by studying horses. For example, horses can teach us that negative behavior can be redirected without confrontation.

If a horse is a kicker or biter or bucker or shier or whatever, I try not to reprimand him when it happens; when performing badly, he would not likely accept my leadership without a battle anyway. I wait and address the problem in an environment where the horse is willing to accept my authority while I redirect him to a new behavior to replace the unwanted behavior. By not pointing out bad behavior, I do not re-enforce it. Eventually the horse will forget the bad behavior because I give it no focus.

Because of the way we take care of horses, they immediately and naturally perceive us as the lead horse. Like a lead horse, we provide them with food, we lead them and we take them new places. We control their movement and behavior. Because of this, a horse sees us as a leader.

If we stay away from disputes and keep the horse's mind focused on our leadership, they automatically accept our authority. If we use aggressive force and bully the horse, we open up the battlefield of resistance. We lower our leadership position and invite pecking order dominance issues. How much better to apply the horse's natural code as a lead horse would, thereby cementing our leadership role and avoiding an ongoing dominance battle.

Magnetic Bond

Once again I will share with you the intricacy of herd behavior. This time we will look at herd behavior to understand why I put so much focus on developing the attitude of horses before I begin traditional training. After looking at the development of a wild horse's behavior, I will share how I develop leadership and magnetism with a horse through the process of getting to know his personality type.

I will start with how foals are shaped by their community, because I shape my relationship with horses in a similar way to how foals are raised by the herd. When I am working with horses, I develop them as if they were children, and I train in stages that are most natural to them. The horse's behavior directs my approach and the stage of his training.

I will point out the stages of social development of a wild horse, to show how it parallels the stages we go through to prepare them to enjoy being ridden or prepare them for competition. This information is designed to give you some ideas in handling your horse in communicating and training. You will learn why you cannot get too aggressive with horses, and the importance focusing on developing horses' strongest instinct, which is to follow a leader, and how to develop a magnetic leadership.

To begin with, since proper herd behavior is so crucial to their survival, horses teach their youngsters early on to follow a leader and to pay attention to the herd and their surroundings. Horses live in a society that must work together to survive predation. Therefore, they are very interactive with each other. Pecking order is how they establish an ability to work together to protect themselves from predators.

I have observed young foals being reprimanded for mean behavior by their elders. The foal initiates his development and lessons from his inappropriate behavior. Once a dominant foal learns guilt for antisocial behavior, he can be put in place with simply a threat in body language. As a foal grows his understanding of body language matures and he begins to pay attention to the leader, community and his surroundings.

It is a learning process that all horses must face. Bratty, dominant behavior puts a foal in jeopardy with predators. It is not good for any horse to become too aggressive because horses are prey animals and the proper amount of fear and respect helps them survive.

The community plays a major part in raising foals. The more aggressive a foal, the more trouble it gets into with older horses. As it continues to grow, it quickly learns that most older horses are going to put it in its place. As the foal matures it becomes more cautious and learns how to win fights in mock fighting games with its buddies. The youngster learns to stay clear of their buddies that can beat them up in the games they play and to fight with the ones that are more their equal. They learn to stay clear of their superiors as well. The young naturally follow a leader from their instinct and from observing that the horses they respect the most follow the leader.

All horses are born with the instinct to follow a leader, and most horses have a desire to be dominant. The instinct to follow a leader is stronger in all horses than their instinct to be dominant because they are herd animals. Even though they are herd animals, horses must learn social skills.

Young horses earn their rank through everyday experimentation from being in the position of authority with some horses in some interactions and being in the position of submission to some horses in other interactions. If a horse is too dominant, he will be curbed by someone in his community. It is a back and forth process.

Maturing horses learn how to be polite, when to follow and when to lead. As they mature, they develop distinct personality types that fall into three main groups: lead, dominant and submissive. Herds are like finishing schools that are ongoing. The horses at the top understand the pecking order better than the ones below them.

The lead horse understands pecking order better than any horse in the band he is leading, but he is not interested in being dominant. He is interested in the herd's survival and keeping the herd unified. Lead horse personality types can be inborn or created by the community. When a lead horse is created by the community and has earned his title, he usually will set his dominant behavior aside to take care of the herd.

When a prospective lead stallion becomes mature, he will leave his original band and focus his interest on collecting a band of mares one by one from other herds and bands. If his leadership skills need more development or he gets too aggressive, his desire to collect mares and those same mares' reaction to him will further his education in more appropriate leadership behavior. He must learn how to develop magnetism.

From his need to be with other horses and his desire to lead a band of mares, he learns how to become desirable as a leader with magnetism. If he isn't desirable to the mares he has collected, he will eventually lose his band. His magnetism is the glue that ultimately keeps his mares with him. When a lead horse has magnetism, horses are drawn to him and have a natural desire to follow his leadership.

Because horses depend on magnetism to be able to function as a leader, I think it is the most important quality humans should develop in working with their horses. I had a natural magnetism with horses, but not as much as a lead horse, so I had to develop what I had. Through my relationship with Mustano and Moonlight, I learned how to develop it. Today, I can draw a horse to me from the horse's desire to be with me. From a horse's desire to be with me, I can develop his desire to accept my leadership just as a lead horse would.

Little has been written on the idea that one can develop magnetism or charisma. Magnetism or charisma is what we think horse whisperers have. We feel people either have magnetism or charisma or they don't. We think charisma is something that happens between humans. To develop charisma with horses, all people have to do is take the time to put themselves in the same circumstances a stallion faces every day keeping his mares happy and in line following his leadership. What is that circumstance? It isn't a round pen. It is in an area that gives the horse you're working with enough room to have the upper hand by being able to escape your influence and leadership if he chooses to.

I develop a relationship with a horse in an area big enough so he can escape my influence. With this circumstance, by knowing how to lead the way a lead horse does, plus a need to get a horse to want my company, points the way to a magical connection. In fact, developing magnetism brings about a better relationship than having magnetism from the very beginning. I was born with it, but I had to learn how to use it.

Building a relationship in a free, open environment is what shaped my leadership behavior. When my leadership behavior was appropriate in this free environment, my magnetism became as strong as a lead stallion's, maybe even stronger, because I did not have the draw a stallion has with his mares. This is why I work horses at liberty in a large area so they have the ability to refuse my leadership and my company, just as mares can refuse the leadership of a stallion by joining another band.

The horse's ability to refuse my relationship makes it possible to distinguish my mistakes in leadership; a horse's reaction lets me know why the horse is rejecting my direction. For example, I could tell a horse's refusals to accept my directions were caused from fear, aggression, boredom or lack of attention by his expression and behavior at the moment he refused my request.

There is another very important factor about giving a horse enough space to get away. If magnetism exists between us in the moment, if a horse is given the ability to control and reject my attempt at leadership, oddly, it develops the horse's interest in accepting my leadership. I remember a proverb that speaks about letting something go that you love, and if you do, it will come back. I remember it being close to how magnetism works. I would rather the proverb say, "if there is love between you at the moment you let it go, it will come back."

Another part of the puzzle of magnetism between horses is reciprocal movement. I discovered that one reason horses are drawn to other horses is that they can affect each other with reciprocal body movement. This is how they build stronger bonds and their opinions of other horses. The horses they are drawn to are the horses they will follow. The more magnetism a horse possesses, the higher his rank if he chooses to take it.

If the conditions in nature are in balance, everything that happens between horses is consenting. Likewise, when a human is working with horses, the magnetism must be established strongly before a person tries to take a leadership role. The horse must choose to be led. If leadership is enforced before the bond, there is not a strong desire to follow. This causes rifts in the relationship between the person and the horse.

The way I begin developing magnetism with a horse is by spending time with him in his paddock or pasture. I want him to feel we are companions. Taking time with a horse to develop his interest to want my companionship is the first stage of my Liberty Training.

The second stage, after the friendship is formed, is "teaching" him to come to me by finding a open spot in the field, standing still and waiting there until he comes. If the experience after he comes to me is enjoyable, I have the beginning stages of magnetism. I put my horses through seven stages that develop extreme magnetism and an enthusiastic performance. The initial bond at liberty increases the horse's performance under saddle to be the best it can be. From this relationship I can develop in the horse a strong work ethic.

Magnetic Leadership Through Reciprocal Movements

A lead horse knows how to use his movements to control the herd. Sometimes they will reciprocate, and sometimes they won't. By using reciprocal movements shared between the herd, the lead horse can gain complete control.

Developing magnetism through reciprocal movements is key to how lead horses develop magnetic leadership. I found that by sharing reciprocal movements, I could create magnetism, loyalty and teamwork by using the same movements that lead horses use. In Book IV, I explain the process of how I gained leadership, respect and cooperation through reciprocal movements.

There are many stories of how people have developed their initial relationship with animals; this is because all people and animals are different. When anyone shares their story with me, I always learn more about the animal mind and a better way to communicate with animals. I will share a particular story with you of a man with infinite wisdom who developed a magnetism with a mature, untrained stallion that seemed unchangeable in his fear and hatred of humans.

When I was in the middle of my breeding and training business, I needed a break and went on vacation to Carmel, California. I took a horse with me for company. His name was Stony. I still have him today. He has been in my life since he was two months old. While on vacation, I worked Stony at liberty everyday and rode him in the hills around the mouth of the valley.

Stony and I had an amazing relationship and our act caught the attention of a well-known horseman by the name of Ray Hackworth. Ray owned the barn where I boarded Stony. Everyday Ray watched me do an exercise with Stony before I rode him. It is an exercise I used to develop my skills in horse communication, like a golfer hitting a bucket of balls to improve his game. I practiced my ability to get Stony to respond to my movements on the ground by driving him away from me and drawing him back to me in an open field; I had to keep him enthusiastic while we practiced. Ray said it reminded him of the beach scene in the movie *The Black Stallion*, when the horse and the boy raced down the beach together and the stallion circled around him, leaping and jumping about.

I had no idea I was being watched until Ray approached me one day and said he was impressed by my relationship with Stony; he was interested in learning more about me and my horsemanship skills. I did not know it then but that was the start of a long friendship. I soon learned that Ray had a great understanding of the importance of "letting nature take its course." He used this way of thinking to develop a relationship with his horses before he started training them and how reciprocal movements develop a bond.

Someone told me that he was in the Cowboy Hall of Fame for his horse training excellence. When I asked him about it, he said he was not in the hall of fame – his horses were. I never learned the details of Ray's connection to the hall of fame, but from what I saw in Ray, I knew it would be a good idea to keep a close eye on how he worked with horses.

Once while in his house, I witnessed Ray discover he had insects in his kitchen. Instead of killing them, he collected every one and put them outside. His house was very clean and tidy and he had his own way about everything he did. He had a soft manner, like his voice. His quiet, pleasant nature gave me the impression there was a lot more to Ray than he was ever going to share with me.

Ray was over sixty at the time and considered himself retired. He liked being around people and had a lot of friends. He was still attractive, both in his looks and his manner. Lean, with thinning gray hair, he was the kind of cowboy who took his hat off if he went into someone's home or needed to talk face-to-face with a lady.

I was in luck when I met him because he had just acquired a Quarter Horse stallion that he was going to be starting under saddle soon. This was a horse that was mean, hated humans and seemed unchangeable. It was an opportunity to learn something about his techniques.

Ray would not tell me anything about what he was doing with his horse. In fact, when I learned how he set the bond with his stallion, he denied that that was what he was doing. I am not sure why he was like that. I learned that Ray took the same interest and time I took to develop a relationship with a horse. He did say that he was "letting nature take its course" and he could not tell how long that would take but when it happened, he would begin riding him.

Ray hung around the stallion's paddock for many weeks just watching him. When I asked why he was spending so much time with his horse, he said that he wasn't spending time with him; he just needed to be there to fix the fence and see how his new horse was doing in his new environment. He carried a hammer and a bucket of nails and every so often would pound a nail or two. When he walked across the paddock and met his horse, he would push the horse out of his path and continue over to the other side and pound another nail. He did that a lot. Sometimes when his horse walked across his paddock, Ray would move out of his way.

He would spend at least an hour a day "fixing" that paddock. I can tell you that nothing needed fixing, but when Ray got finished with all that "repair work," that wild stallion that had never liked people, liked him. The stallion's jumpy nature and flinching side when you approached him was gone and he was happy to place his head in a halter – Ray had developed a bond with him. "Fixing" that paddock was enough interaction and time for "letting nature take its course."

It was important for me to see Ray sharing reciprocal movements with the stallion just like I do in my Liberty Training, Beyond the Whisper™, and like horses do with each other in the wild. Time and reciprocal movements brought Ray and his stallion to a friendship; from the reciprocal movements they developed a language that only Ray and his horse understood. I could see when the magnetism was totally in place between them, and so could everyone else. When the stallion became comfortable with Ray, he became comfortable with other people as well.

I was fortunate to see a true master at work and learn what he felt was important, even if it was to just see him pound a few nails every day. The reason he would not admit what he was doing probably had to do with the cowboy culture he grew up in. I think if he had admitted to me his real purpose in "fixing the paddock," it would have opened the door to press him for more information.

Ray was uncomfortable talking about horse training. Every time I brought up the subject, he slipped out of it by claiming, "I never trained a horse to do anything. I was just lucky enough to ride a couple of 'super stars.'" Oddly though, every horse he stepped onto always shined in its performance. Ray once told me, "I'm not really a very good trainer. It's just that my horses like me a lot."

Ray and I spent all day together most of my vacation. He was as interested in watching me train as I was in watching him work a cow and pound nails. I called what I did with horses "play" and he called what he did "luck." However either of us termed what we did with our horses before we rode them, I consider it good horsemanship. And it is not out of the realm of anyone else's ability.

Anyone can do "what comes naturally," what Ray and I were doing at liberty. But they won't even try it if they don't understand how important it is to interact with their horse in this simple way – sharing time and space everyday like horses do with each other, moving a horse around, letting him move you around, easy and gentle like, with lots of pauses in between. Reciprocal movements are important to animals. It is largely how they communicate with each other. Even different species can communicate with each other in this manner. Such simple things bring about such a powerful bond that I just had to share it!

Ray has since passed on. He gave me an antique Visalia hand-tooled parade saddle with rawhide lacing that I still remember him by. Where Ray put his focus validates how important it is to share a magnetic connection with a horse before you ask him to accept your authority and leadership. The relationship he developed in the paddock "fixing the fence," as Ray would put it, created a language and bond between him and his horse. "Letting nature take its course" in shared harmonious moments works with horses as well as it did in the harmonious moments of companionship that Ray and I shared.

Shaping Behavior in the Bond and Keeping the Connection

Unfortunately, most people don't have to worry about how much magnetism they have with their horse. Nor do they think it is important. They don't need magnetism to lead and ride a horse. They don't turn their horse loose in nature and use magnetism to bring him back. Because people don't work a horse in a free environment where the horse can accept or reject their leadership, they don't even get a chance to develop this quality.

Horses are kept confined and controlled with halters, ropes and bridles. All a person must worry about is keeping the horse willing to perform. But this can sometimes be difficult, especially with young horses. If the person develops magnetism with a horse first and develops leadership in a free-choice environment, the horse will be much easier to handle and the person's horsemanship skills will be more advanced.

Handling and riding horses at any level of relationship, from professional to back yard owner, requires a certain amount of natural ability. Anyone who enjoys riding horses has an innate ability. To ride a horse you must have leadership skills, communication skills and, from my view point, even a certain amount of magnetism. Few people possess the magnetism it takes to shape a horse to want to perform enthusiastically what they ask of him. The good news is that between leadership ability, communication skills, and magnetism, the easiest ability to develop is magnetism.

Without developing a magnetic relationship with your horse, it takes longer to develop your horsemanship skills in horse training. Without magnetism, it takes years to develop the skill of getting a horse to move off pressure and keep the horse willing in the process. Moving off pressure is a horse training term to describe the aids we use on horses to get them to perform. For example, if we take up the reins, the horse should slow down or stop, depending on how much pressure he experiences. If we asked a horse to go forward, the pressure to the horse would come from our leg aids.

Once people learn this system, it works very well for them and their world of horses becomes a world of asking and correcting; magnetism is set aside. Proper correction, direction and authority is all that is needed. The negative aspect of this way of handling horses is that it can create a situation where the only reward to the horse is an absence of pressure.

Horses take to being captured and corrected very well – perhaps too well. Horses respond so well to this system that magnetism is not used. However, when we see true magnetism between a horse and rider, we would all love to have that connection.

The reason horses respond to correction by humans so well is that they are constantly on the lookout for overaggressive behavior and correct it when it occurs within the herd. Correction, in a horse's mind, is an attempt to restore community harmony in the wild – it is an honorable job. Because it works so well, it often gets misused by humans. All too often communication becomes only a tool of correction, demanding not asking, and moving away from pressure becomes the only reason for a horse to perform.

Moving away from pressure is a good tool if we are careful not to overcorrect. It works well with horses, but it works even better if we start with a magnetic connection with our horse. From a magnetic connection, a horse is more willing and correction is less necessary. This ensures that moving off pressure doesn't turn into abuse.

A horse's motivation to perform shouldn't be simply to move away from pressure. It is better to get a horse to feel a sense of accomplishment and pride in his performance if he is a show horse and a sense of partnership as a riding horse. It is better to develop a horse's taste for what he is doing. It is important to build desire in the horse to want to perform. By giving more attention to developing the horse's taste for what he is doing, control is gained through the horse's desire rather than submission through correction and moving off pressure.

It takes time to develop magnetism with a horse. It takes more time in the beginning stages to set the bond so that a person has a solid foundation to build upon. This extra time to set the bond will decrease the time it takes to fully train the horse. We need to develop our relationship with a horse in a way that is most natural to him.

When the bond is established, I am able to shape his personality and develop his enthusiasm. When the horse is shaped to follow his instinct and desire, it creates a partnership for the optimum teamwork I am looking for under saddle in the future.

In the relationship between horse and human before the bond is set, there are a number of ongoing problems that we will be addressing. Because dominant horses enjoy pecking order games of who is dominant, they need to be kept in check even when they are totally in our charge. Because of this, they need daily shaping. When we interact with a horse, the horse will judge each interaction from his point of view and respond accordingly.

If a horse sees a person's behavior in a specific interaction as a lead horse behavior, he will typically perform what he is being asked to perform. If he sees a person's behavior as a submissive horse behavior, he will try to direct you. If he sees a person's behavior as a dominant horse behavior, he will almost always question your authority. The only time that this is not so is once you have established a deep bond with a horse and a commitment to accept your leadership.

Once you acquire this deep spiritual bond, a horse will naturally follow your leadership from the magnetism you share with him. There are all kinds of bonds; the strongest bond is the one that is formed through spending time with a horse and reciprocal movements to establish leadership that a horse respects and enjoys. The bond I am speaking of is readily seen with children and their horses, at the racetrack with horses and their grooms and, of course, in movies like *The Black Stallion* and *Fury*.

Once the bond is in place, when a horse exhibits undesirable behavior but at the same time feels affection for me, I can then shape the horse to the behavior I desire. I don't shape behavior if he is angry and doesn't feel friendly toward me at the time because, at that moment, the magnetism for keeping him with me would be gone. He would accept correction in a negative way.

There are two parts to the bond: One is the passive time I spend with a horse; the other is the interactive time I spend. There must be a balance for the relationship to be at its best.

I work with a horse in two stages every day. First, I spend time with the horse in the moment in passive time. When I get the feeling that he has connected to me in friendship and is focused on me, I begin with my daily program, whether it is riding him or traditional training. Sometimes the passive time I spend is as short as a quick hello from my horse. If he comes up to me, gives me a sniff and places his head in the halter, he is ready to go. (Putting on a halter is a critical time. If the horse objects to being haltered, it will negatively affect the interactions you have with him thereafter.)

If I am working with a horse on a regular basis, the longest time before putting him to work is usually about 15 minutes. In every case, spending the extra time paid off.

Each day, the sign that a horse is ready and the bond is in place is that he will volunteer to place his head in the halter. From this first stage of waiting for the glue to set between us, a kind of connection of friendship occurs. When I can feel this connection, I begin interacting with a horse. Until this happens, I do not have a consenting horse.

After working with a horse, I spend as much down time with him as working time. I might keep him with me while I am saddle soaping tack or doing other chores, or I turn him out on a green pasture to graze and keep him company. Instead of putting him on a hot walker, I hand walk him. At my training facility, we hand walk our horses every time we work them because of the connection of friendship and obedience it creates.

Once the bond is set, I focus my training on shaping behavior by curbing dominant behavior or soothing fearful behavior. I accomplish this through Liberty Training, Beyond the Whisper™, or hand walking around the school or on a trail. I am looking to shape a horse's behavior to be in a range between the extremes of being too dominant or too fearful. Interestingly, the lead horse's behavior falls in this range.

After many years of training, I found that lead horses do not need daily shaping like dominant and submissive horses. This is because after the bond is in place, lead horses give up their interest in squabbling and are more interested in caretaking and facilitating humans. They are service oriented and love being given a job. Lead horses are not fearful or aggressive; they are team players when treated with respect.

In several tests of character that I have witnessed or directed myself, I have found that lead horses are very different than dominant horses. When lead stallions were put together artificially in a fenced field, their behavior was completely different than all other types of horse personalities. They did not fight to set their order. With no visible sign of how they came to their decisions, they established their rank and order in such a short time that it appeared like they knew their place from the very beginning.

From lead horse behavior and how horses go about developing unity from daily shaping other horses' behavior, I put what I learned into practice. I came to the conclusion that there are two reasons for daily shaping: First, for shaping a horse to be more like a lead horse – not too dominant or fearful, and second, for a horse that may need social interaction for emotional well-being. Like people, horses need a certain amount of social interaction to be well adjusted.

From daily shaping, dominant horses can be brought to think like a lead horse. My interest is not to take a dominant horse to a lower position in the pecking order. Instead, I teach him that he cannot lower my position. After he has a clear understanding of my personal rights, I get him to think like a leader. By that I mean I develop his interest to take direction like a lead horse.

Instead of moving the dominant horse down the pecking order ladder, I move him up. I first correct the overly dominant behavior like a lead horse would, and then I give him a request. When a dominant horse is in the right frame of mind or has been put in his place (remembering the bond is set), at that moment he will be in the mood to perform what is asked of him. Allowing him to perform at the moment I know he would perform rather than forcing him to perform lets him feel a sense of control, which is very important for a dominant horse; it builds his ego. From the enjoyment of being in charge of a job well done, he develops a service mentality like a lead horse.

Submissive horses need shaping as well. Their focus is lacking and they need to be constantly brought back to attention. In the wild, submissive horses are picked on for forgetting to maintain reciprocal movements in relationship with the horses around them. Of course, submissive horses cannot be made to become lead horses, but by building their interest and confidence, I can develop them to have more attention through developing their ability to be powerful.

At liberty, I build confidence in a submissive horse in a training situation. With the horse moving around with me in slow or fast gaits, I move out of his way. In short order, the horse begins to notice that I am behaving as if I am afraid of his presence. When he notices this, he will start experimenting by deliberately coming into my space. When he does, I jump out of his way. I keep this up until the horse becomes rude by threatening me with his ears back, demanding that I get out of his way. When I am sure the horse has lots of confidence, I make a correction to let him know that his behavior has gone over the top. From this game, the horse develops much more focus and confidence; from this attitude the horse is much more willing and manageable.

Each day the horse develops more and more confidence. I have to work submissive horses in faster gaits because their energy is usually low. Faster gaits build their energy. This is my first interest. I get the horse to move quickly and then when it comes anywhere close to me, I move out of the way. Soon the submissive horse moves up the pecking order ladder. At that time I praise the horse with "good boy!" or "good girl!" and in no time at all, I have a horse that wants to learn and perform. It is confident and willing.

Working a horse without tack in a space where he feels a sense of freedom and personal power and a desire to be with me is exciting for the horse and myself. At the moment we are connected in movements in companionship interactions, the horse is in a state of "Naked Liberty." In those moments I am in true harmony with my horse and the performance we are sharing together.

Beyond a perfect performance comes the unbridled spirit. In this state, tack can be used as a communication line rather than for controlling the horse against his will, trapping his expression. I use my Liberty Training, Beyond the Whisper™ method daily to build the connection I will need to get an optimum performance under saddle. Daily Liberty Training gains the horse's permission, attention and desire to perform.

The information I have learned about herd behavior helps me instruct and explain how to communicate with horses. I have been able to pass on to other people my natural gift with horses. Not everyone can develop this ability, but most people can come miles closer to a more rewarding relationship with their horse just from wanting to.

As a horse trainer, the compassion I have for animals and my sensitivity to their rights of personal space and behavior is where I put my focus because I have a strong natural leadership ability. People's problems with horses stem from not knowing how to be a team player and a leader at the same time. When this ability is developed, magnetism will bloom.

A common mistake people make is believing that if their horse likes them, he will do what they want him to do. This leads them to baby their horse too much. On the other hand, some keep their horse under control with a strong upper hand but give no attention to the relationship. Both extremes need to be brought to a balance. What works is paying attention to the horse so you can make adjustments in how you lead, in order to have your horse respond positively. Never believe that you can stop being a leader. You cannot expect your horse to perform without proper direction on your part.

When I work with a horse, my interest is to keep the unity by keeping him focused on performing. I focus on shaping the horse's behavior when he is in my charge. I keep his attention on me at all times by asking him to perform a job, for example, to stand on a loose rein or to eat grass while I am talking to a friend. I don't let my horse tell me he is going to eat grass. I tell him he has my permission. If he tries to eat grass without my permission, I ask him to stand on a dropped rein at attention instead. If he can't do that for me, I don't talk with my friend. Instead, I keep walking to keep his focus and my leadership in place. I don't ask a horse to perform a task he is not ready to perform. I choose a task I know he would do.

The most important tools people have working with horses are, in this order, 1) feeling comfortable around them, 2) having a natural leadership ability, 3)interacting with them using the bond to develop magnetism, and 4) making correct leadership decisions that lead to optimum performance. If you feel comfortable around your horse, you have the ability to develop a bond. If you have natural leadership ability, you can learn to make the correct leadership decisions.

I hope that what I have shared gives you some ideas on how to interact with your horse and that you might be empowered by a better understanding of the mind of horses and how they respond; of how to deal with personality types of horses to work in partnership; and of the importance of keeping the bond in place.

A Better Communication System Through Pecking Order

I learned from horses that through the pecking order process, they acquire a superior communication system. This system of communication is a connection that is truly magical. I discovered that when my students establish a relationship with a horse the way horses do, using the pecking order rituals to establish rank, they acquire the ability to communicate with their horses with the same ability the horses have with each other. To reveal more insight into the mind of a horse, leadership and pecking order, I will go back to my observations with Mustano and Moonlight to show how this phenomenal telepathic communication is formed.

My interest was clearly focused on the everyday life of Mustano and Moonlight in regard to where they put their attention. Moonlight spent much of her time focused on the entire band. She wanted the band to stay focused on where she was at all times. She threatened a horse with a bite or kick if it did not keep an eye on her. Between Mustano breaking up battles and Moonlight keeping the horses alert, the community was well tended.

From Mustano with his band of mares, I learned that leadership behavior is a good thing when it supports the well-being of each individual and keeps the peace. I could see dominant horses wanting to be led when Mustano led them back to their kinder ways and checked them for their bad behavior. Such leadership gives dominant horses security. It reminds dominant horses of their relationship with their mothers and of the games they played growing up.

Horses by nature are socially curious and are always looking to fit in and then move up. The moving up happens when another horse higher on the pecking order is not paying attention. This is why humans need to stay focused on their horses. Testing power is in the nature of horses; winning or losing position is a natural part of young horses' social growth. Because this jockeying for position is such a natural part of horse behavior, horses find it easy to forgive humans their mistakes in their leadership interactions with horses.

In the basic nature of horses, the strongest desire is to be with other horses. The horse they like the best, other than their best friend, is the lead horse they have chosen to follow. Dominant horses feel secure, and even nurtured, being led. This is why it is so important for humans to focus their attention on shaping a dominant horse's respect. When we do, he will like us better.

I also learned that pecking order is a good thing because of the results it creates. A well-seasoned herd that jostles for rights and position results in a band of leaders of leaders. When they have arrived at this relationship, pecking order is over; they are a united front. The jostling ceases and friendships are stable. From the fabric of these conditions spring a one-mind consciousness and shared movements in harmony. When pecking order among horses finally drops out as a communication system, it is replaced by a bond, and a new communication system is born.

Their instinct guides them to search for the bond because within the bond lies their strength, safety, well-being and superior communication system. When the bond is in place, the highest form of communication is born within the herd – a communication system similar to telepathy.

I felt that if a horse could develop a relationship with me the same way he would with another horse, I would acquire this telepathic communication system. I felt the secret to acquiring this connection for communication was to avoid getting caught up in the pecking order aspect and instead to set the rules of antisocial behavior. I could get to the bond much faster with less dominant pecking order behavior by acting like a lead horse. Again, working with horses is not about being tough or sweet; it is about shaping behavior. Perhaps the best way to see what I am talking about is to look at a big problem to see how to deal with a small one.

I'm going to share a story about a horse named Serpico who was antisocial with other horses. Serpico took leadership skills to the extreme. He was a dominant gelding that never bothered other horses unless they picked a fight, and if they did, he had a way with words that set his rivals straight. Of course his words were body language, power, timing and a passion for being left alone. He was a different kind of horse because he was antisocial with other horses. He was an Arabian liver chestnut, often times mistaken for black. He was thin-skinned, about 16 hands tall. That was tall for an Arabian back in the early 70s. He looked more Thoroughbred than Arabian.

Every morning, when I fed him in his field, I would find him running for exercise. He ran as if he were racing against a phantom horse he loved to beat. The food I gave him would not stop him from running. I watched him racing around his two-acre field as if he were in a competition. At some point in his pasture, as if he had reached the finish line, he would break into a lope, slow down, turn around and walk back to his food. He would start eating like a winner eating a breakfast for champions.

He was a high-spirited, dominant horse, afraid of nothing. Had there been something for him to be afraid of, he would have been, but nothing ever came into his life that challenged him. He looked at everything as entertainment except other horses' company.

One day I drove a pickup truck into his pasture and he promptly jumped up into the bed for the fun of it. Teaching him how to load was certainly not necessary. He was just as willing the first time I rode him. He liked being ridden so well that I could imagine him saddling himself and asking me to get on.

He was named after the movie *Serpico*. The movie was about a famous cop from New York named Serpico. He came with that name when I bought him as a long yearling at the time I had just opened my training and breeding business. It seemed odd that his name was Serpico. Whoever named him could not have guessed that Serpico's main job throughout his life was to be my police horse.

In the years I had a training business, instead of dealing with nasty dominant behavior in horses that had come to be fixed, I would turn them loose with my old standby gelding, Serpico. It was Serpico's job to set the horse to better behavior so I would not have to address the problem.

Serpico had his own style for fixing undesirable behavior in other horses. When I turned a new horse loose, he would ignore the horse. If the horse stayed away from him, he would leave the other horse alone. He was not interested in any relationship with other horses. He would even let a horse eat with him from the same hay pile to avoid having to acknowledge his presence. Because Serpico allowed horses to eat with him, mean dominant horses would try to pick fights with him at the hay pile. That is where they made their mistake. No horse Serpico ever ran across could beat him up, but he never hurt another horse too badly. He knew how to intimidate and could get a horse to the ground and not let him up. Horses very quickly learned to stay clear of him.

When the new horse had gone through the school of Serpico, what he had learned about respect and proper table manners translated over to respecting me as well. It is amazing how much a horse's overall attitude changes when his realizes that eating is a privilege and territory belongs to someone else.

Horses often came to the ranch with behavior problems like crowding, stepping on peoples toes, biting, kicking, tacking up and even riding issues. Once they had experienced Serpico's discipline, their problems were much easier to correct. When a dominant horse came to the barn still nasty after a stint with Serpico, I would return them to Serpico for a second treatment. No horse ever had to go back a third time.

Sometimes people had made a horse so mean that when the horse came to be fixed and I turned him loose with Serpico, he would rip out of his halter to attack Serpico. It made no difference to Serpico how aggressive a horse was; the result was the same. In seconds,

Serpico would have him on the ground and scared to death.

Serpico had a formula that worked every time. He would keep a horse in a position of surrender on the ground until he felt the horse was entirely submissive. Then he would let him up and walk away as if what had happened was no big deal.

Serpico clearly loved people and children but had no use for other horses. Even with his antisocial need to be left alone, he had a big heart. Although he had the power and strength to seriously injure any horse, he never, ever crossed the line with me or any other person. Un-gelded in the wild, he probably would have been very social and a great leader of leaders. Gelding changed his allegiance from horses to humans.

He was truly a different kind of guy, and was excellent with children and in programs for the handicapped. He would, however, show aggressive behavior toward people who tried to force him against his will. But he had a good mom – me – and we never had any problems with each other. Serpico was the safest horse I ever owned, he had his own way of keeping the peace, and his name suited him perfectly.

My relationship with wild horses is what gave me the courage to trust my instincts using Serpico. No one should try this police horse idea unless they have a good sense of reading the personality of both horses and have enough room for the horses to run and stay away from each other. Horse fights can be fatal. Never turn horses loose together with shoes on.

Today, when I work with aggressive or negative behavior, I don't have to get the horse to the ground like my big guy Serpico, because I learned what worked for him: The horse is not allowed to eat his food when he is aggressive. So there is where I put my effort. With a very difficult horse, I teach him to run from my company first without food through my aggressive body language and by advancing in his direction at a time that he would naturally run way from me.

I practice this flight exercise in his paddock until it becomes automatic and routine. Then I put down food – something he would eat but not enjoy or savor so much that it might bring out more aggression. When he goes over to eat it, I chase him away. When he gives up interest in eating, I go over and pet him and lead him back to the hay. From this exercise alone, the angry horse learns polite behavior. Being polite turns him back to being social and fair in his overall behavior.

I have worked with horses so dangerous that at first I would not even get into the corral with them. I got the job done by using a fence to keep me safe from aggressive attacks. I offer them food and as long as they are gentle, I feed them. When they try to tear the food from me, I don't let them have it. Little by little they learn that they need to work with me. Any time a horse understands that he can work with you, he loses his antisocial behavior, just like people.

From watching wild horses throughout my life, I have seen what horses do all day in nature. Often times horses reprimand each other for all kinds of infractions. A horse that is frightened by something he doesn't need to fear may be met with a bite or kick from another horse. These infractions and their punishments are going on all the time. Horses even enjoy pushing each other around as a pleasurable pastime before they become an established herd.

Patterning my leadership after Mustano, I learned to stay away from these kinds of reprimands and went about shaping the horses focus on what I wanted him to do. From Mustano I learned that to reprimand effectively, I needed to make a big statement, but without pain.

From these experiences with Mustano and his band, it was evident that within a balanced dynamic of lead horse, dominant horses and submissive horses, there is perfect community in teamwork. The lead horse protects the herd, keeps the peace and sets the direction of the herd. The dominant horses, through their need to keep their place in rank, cause the herd to stay alert to danger. Their need for order creates a chain of command that a lead horse can direct. The submissive horses add safety to the herd by their numbers.

This balance is created by many elements, such as a need to stay together to survive, enough land to get away from an aggressive horse and the ability to leave a herd and find another. A horse's personality and herd instincts are most important to his ability to fit in with a herd. Without an ability to fit in, the ability to survive is greatly lessened. Safety in numbers plays an important role to an individual's well-being.

I believe that over time these three personality types were created as nature culled those traits that did not support the survival of the herd; horses that were too dominant and unwilling to follow a leader, horses that had no interest in pecking order, and horses that were too submissive. The flaw these misfits had in common was a lack of herd instinct.

Lead, dominant and submissive personalities know when to follow and when to lead. This behavior is key to their survival. These three personalities work so well together because no matter what personality type, they share the same herd instinct, namely, the ability to fit in. This ability to fit in creates a unity that is admirable and has personally captured my attention.

Pecking order is more of a need for order and harmony than a survival of the fittest. The broader aspect of pecking order is that it develops the horses' language and communication systems to a one-mind consciousness. It is most important for horsemen to understand this. Understanding pecking order from this perspective allows us to create a sense of well-being in a horse and form a spiritual bond that can continue to grow and mature.

By understanding herd instinct, one can develop a connection with horses and the ability to train them. The idea of training, at this point, seems almost against what is natural because we so admire the wild horse's spirit. But as we start training a horse by creating a voluntary performance without force, we enter the horse's world. He begins to teach us through shaping our leadership behavior and developing our understanding of teamwork and communication. In this approach, the horse is not the reluctant teacher, but our guide.

A horse is more comfortable with humans who know how to lead. It is not about being sweet or being aggressive. It is about keeping a horse focused on staying connected to his instinct to follow a leader. It is our job to be the kind of leader he would enjoy following.

If a horseman has a way of thinking that is in harmony with his horse, it draws his horse to join him in teamwork. The essence of gaining a spiritual connection with a horse is that you develop a natural ability to lead, and the horse has a natural desire to follow. Understanding pecking order and how lead horses lead provides the magical map.

Carolyn Resnick

Book Four

The language of
movement,
communication
and leadership
through the ways
of horses.

Carolyn Resnick

Chapter XXIV
Two Worlds Walking
Permission from My Elders

Before I start my unbroken story of being accepted into a wild horse herd and riding Moonlight from a bonded trust, it is important for me to share my spiritual study program from Verde Valley School in Sedona, Arizona. Verde Valley School was a college preparatory boarding school where I spent my freshman year of high school. The school gave me an ability to find wisdom in the passion I had for horses. This knowledge gave me the impetus to share with others the important information about developing better unity and teamwork through what I learned from horses. As a child I could have been guided to pick a career with financial security, as children were encouraged to do in those days, instead of inventing a career that fit my abilities. However, the school showed me the spiritual importance of following my interests and instincts. They pointed out that my passion for horses had produced leadership insight that was vital to the community of humankind. Without my experience at Verde Valley School, I would not have understood the important part I could play from my spiritual connection with horses. From what I had learned from horses, I could develop a longing in humans to be in harmony with their community and develop their teamwork and leadership skills through better communication that would support each individual.

From my experiences in nature, I learned how to establish a bond and a unified connection with wild horses. I discovered that there is a process that must be followed to gain leadership. I learned of this process by communicating with wild horses in their world, on their terms and to their spirit. I had already found a bridge from the world of horses to my own. Verde Valley School taught me how to apply that bridge to benefit the community of humankind.

Sedona, Arizona – October 28, 1956

I cracked open the window of my dorm room and gazed out at the rain angling down and across the valley and the rainbow bridges jumping from intermittent showers to bright sunlight.

My bag was packed. I was ready to go. This would be my first trip away from the red, red world of Sedona, Arizona, away from the cluster of white stucco buildings that made up Verde Valley High School. For our first intercultural studies assignment, the freshman class was going to spend more than ten days on a Hopi reservation.

Verde Valley was a small boarding school in the high desert. I was glad to be attending, even if only for a year. For one thing, Verde Valley had an equestrian program, which meant I had been able to bring my horse with me to campus. For another, the focus at Verde Valley was on anthropology; they offered a Native American Studies program that included intercultural experiences throughout Mexico and Arizona. American Indians had a way with horses and that they saw the spirit in nature and understood the community we share with the earth and its denizens.

I believed in a common thread that binds all creatures together through their need for community and social structure. I intended to center my studies on the meaning of community and cultural behavior. By walking with horses, I had learned much about the human community. By studying the community of humankind, I hoped to gain a deeper understanding of the community of horses.

To prepare us for our encounter with the Hopi community, our humanities teacher, Joe Brown (known to some as "Lame Deer" and the apprentice of Black Elk), gave our class an exercise in meditation on point-of-view. He had us sit in a large circle with an acorn in the center. We were told to sit silently and look at the acorn for an hour. In that hour, we were to study the acorn thoroughly. When the exercise was over, we would ask our classmates what we had seen.

When it was my turn to speak, I gave a detailed report, as factual as possible. I attached not a single metaphor to my oration even though I wanted to. I made no mention of live oak trees, centuries, universes, or the power a small acorn. I wanted to impress Joe with my ability to see what was truly before me without coloring it with my opinions.

It wouldn't have mattered if I had. It turned out Joe was not interested in what any of us saw. In fact, he wasn't even interested in the acorn. He only wanted us to see that each of our stories was different. He said that everything each of us felt was different. He said none of us love the same way, or suffer the same way – we even experience pain differently. Nothing we share on this earth is the same from one person to another, except for one thing, and the one thing we had in common was loneliness. The loneliness we feel hurts the same in all of us and never goes away. Loneliness binds us together in community and makes us all equal. No one's loneliness hurts more or less than anyone else's.

I left the classroom that day as if I had been reborn. For the first time in my life I felt a deep sense of community with all of human-kind, and this feeling has never left me. Even today, if I encounter someone who looks down on me, I will look that person eye-to-eye, because I see his pain and know that our need for each other is deep.

Joe explained our current assignment by saying it was the respon-sibility of each student to get to know a Hopi family. He warned us we would not likely share a common language with our hosts and, in fact, he hoped that would be the case. If our behavior was polite and respectful, a family would invite us to live in their home. At the end of the assignment, we would write about our experience and de-scribe how we went about establishing a relationship with our hosts.

As soon as I heard about the assignment, I was excited. When I was seven I started collecting Kachinas – small, finely-crafted dolls that I had heard the Hopi used as teaching aids for their children – and ever since then, I had wanted to meet a Hopi spiritual leader. This was going to be my chance.

I talked to Joe about my dream. The only real information he was willing to share was where I might find the spiritual leader – living on his own, just outside of the community. But Joe cautioned me that my goal would be hard to accomplish. I was not permitted to address the spiritual leader unless he spoke to me first. Even then, I would have to maintain silence except to answer direct questions or to say, "Thank you." It would be a great honor if the spiritual leader did speak to me, Joe agreed, but if the spiritual leader didn't … what was I going to do about my paper? He suggested I consider the consequences. My grade would suffer greatly if I spent all my time on the reservation and failed to learn anything about the Hopi people and their customs. I started to ask too many questions and Joe said, "The desert should not be a good place for those who do not believe in the ways of nature." He went on to say, "When questions are asked from doubt and disbelief, answers are not ever good enough."

Joe's warnings didn't daunt my resolve, though. My shyness and tenacity were an advantage in getting along with horses, but in my own world with humans, these characteristics were a hindrance. I was too shy to approach a Hopi family and win an invitation from them. In a way, it seemed more natural to keep quiet until someone spoke to me directly. All I had to do was figure out how to meet the Hopi spiritual leader under circumstances that would give him a good reason to talk to me. I needed a plan – but it would have to wait until I got to the Hopi Community at Second Mesa.

We made the journey to the reservation in a small caravan of four green, box-like, cattle trucks with windows. Each was packed with students, teachers, food and supplies, camping gear, notebooks and pens. We were a jigsaw puzzle in a sardine can, layers of legs and feet and bodies interlocked in a once-in-a-lifetime experience. Our only luxury was two rows of windows, so those standing could look out as well as those sitting on the floor. For much of the trip, nobody bothered to look out at all – the truck kicked up so much dirt, we couldn't see through the windows. If students managed to doze, ruts in the road would soon bounce them awake and hurl the lot of us to the floor of the flatbed. We'd regroup, rearrange ourselves and sit in cautious anticipation of the next sudden jolt. We all agreed the ride was a wonderful adventure.

As we bumped and rattled along the dirt road, I gazed between the billows of dust, scanning the flat and silent land around us. We had left the world of fast cars and modern conveniences far behind us. Telephone poles were the last signs of civilization. When they disappeared, there was nothing left but flat ground, rocks and nameless bushes.

I knew it was strange to many of my classmates, but for me, the world beyond our truck held the only feeling that was truly familiar to me. Without my family, without my horses, far from home, my inner strength came from a secret I shared with no one. Outside was my world – the desert. Out there was freedom in a place I felt comfortable. Joe Brown had told me that Native American children are never left alone. My childhood experience was just the opposite, so I was already in culture shock being in a truck full of kids and we hadn't even reached the reservation.

Four and a half hours and one hundred twenty miles later, we reached our destination, Second Mesa, at about a 6,000-foot elevation. I was sure that for most of the Verde Valley students – especially the ones from New England – the desert would be their greatest challenge. They would feel displaced and frightened in this vast, dry, strange land until they found security with a Hopi family. But as Joe had taught us, we each tell a different story. Though the trip had been fun, by the time we reached our destination, I'd had all the community I needed for one day. I needed to find comfort from things that were familiar to me: the desert, space and solitude.

The day had cleared the clouds. It wasn't even cold. There was a quietness I had never felt before and a clarity that chased away all my thoughts except the few I needed for attending to my duties. Everyone seemed to be experiencing the same feelings. We were at the end of the world and at the beginning of understanding another culture, community and people.

We walked up to the Hopi community. It was no more than a quarter mile from where the trucks were parked and where camp would be for those of us who didn't find a family. Just outside the village, we were met by a group of Hopi children. They greeted us, but not very pleasantly. It was clear we were going to have to earn respect from these kids. It wouldn't be easy.

I headed out of town. There I found a house that just possibly was the Hopi spiritual leader's home. I walked past it and continued out into the desert.

Just a few hundred yards from the house, I came upon a small hill. I climbed to the top of the hill. I could see the desert in all directions, though it didn't seem reasonable that such a little hillock could command such a dramatic view. There were no mountains to crowd the sky. There was more sky than earth. It circled the earth like a blue dome. The hill exposed the desert's vastness; the distinctions and subtleties filled me with a sense of awe.

I spent the rest of the afternoon on the hill, laying my plans for the days ahead. From my lookout I could see the small house of the Hopi spiritual leader. I could also see that he would be able to see me from his porch.

Somehow I knew that this hill was my best and only solution. I felt my approach to meeting the Hopi spiritual leader and getting him to speak to me had to include this hill. It was very small – as small as my request – though I sensed it contained tremendous power. The Hopi spiritual leader's house was to the northwest; he could see me watch the sun rise and set each day. The days would be long with no mountains to shorten the daylight, but I would wait and watch from this hill, turning my face to the sun until it disappeared beneath the horizon.

As each new day broke, I would go out to the hill, then back to the camp for lunch and a leisurely siesta, then out to the hill again, then back to camp after the sun had set. I walked back and forth in front of the spiritual leader's house four times every day. Even though the hill was not too far from the trucks or the community, I felt I was hundreds of miles away from everyone. Joe's teachings on meditation were creating a feeling of emptiness and I felt for the first time a deep sense of loss.

During my second day, horrible thoughts began to enter my mind. What if the Hopi spiritual leader didn't speak English? What if I had the wrong house? Then I remembered that Joe had told me that questions created doubt, so I let go of my questions. I joined in the desert's solitude until I, too, became still. There was no place to be, only here.

I got to know the hill as I waited to be accepted by a world of which I knew nothing, a world for which I had no gifts. I sat on the round hill looking at the horizon. The sky was like the sea as it lays claim to the edge of the shore. The hill spoke to me clearer than dancing horses or the words of my own kind.

Days passed and self-awareness surged through me. I struggled with my identity and ego. Until now, I had always looked to find myself in the things around me, in the family of horses, in school, in books, in my religious studies. I had always sought to find myself in my egotistical, idealistic philosophy of life.

Now I found myself looking within to know who I was and discovering ... nothing. There was nothing at all in me. Nothing worth honoring, nothing new, nothing unexpected – except boredom. My ego was growing smaller and smaller. I felt sad and lonely. Oddly, my experience on the hill brought up emotions of joy, fear, loneliness and a new feeling for me: boredom. It made no sense to me.

Wrestling with my boredom and the moment, I began to fear that what I was doing was of no consequence. Self-doubt gave me a new reason to meet the Hopi spiritual leader. I needed a sign from him, an acknowledgement that I wasn't fooling myself. I needed to be affirmed in my belief that my dedication to horses had a purpose. I needed him to tell me that what I had learned by living in community with horses was of benefit to the community of mankind – to our well-being and the spirit of peaceful coexistence.

Instead of feeling bored, I began to feel lost. Staring at the desert's vastness, minutes turned to hours and each hour was longer than the last.

And suddenly it happened. I started noticing the space between my thoughts, between my feelings, the space between my breaths, the space in myself, vast as the desert. I found the void, the empty place within myself, in the land and sky and universe. I found the black hole that swallows everything, the nothing that connects all things past, present and future. It is the void that gives birth to all things.

As the winds swept across the desert and the whispering breeze played in the nameless bushes and in my hair, a boundless distance danced with solitude and then for a moment time stopped … I could see myself, sitting on the hill.

It was the end of my last day at Second Mesa. I had faced the days without distraction to prove my courage. I had held my loneliness like a sad child needing comfort from another soul and bravely feeling the companionship of one.

Before leaving the hill for the last time, I said, "Thank you" to the hill, the sky, the desert and the Hopi people. Waiting for the Hopi spiritual leader had brought me to a synchronous awareness of joy and suffering. I gained a new meaning of the words freedom and peace. I developed an awareness of sorrow when there is joy, an awareness of joy when there is sorrow, a place to be when there are no words or thoughts.

I buried my palms into the sand of the hill for the last time, saying goodbye, then got up and brushed my hands together to clean them off and wipe them on my jeans. I started my walk back.

I had walked by the Hopi spiritual leader's house every morning, every noon and every evening. He was usually on his porch. He was there today. I walked past him like a soldier, looking out at the desert as if there was nothing else to look at. I hoped he would understand my love of the sky and land. I hoped he might understand also that my vigil on the hill had been a ceremony, a ritual to gain his permission to meet with him. After more than ten days I had run out of time. With only a few minutes left, soon it would all be over.

He called out to me.

I turned and faced him. I walked up to him, then stopped, peering at him, frozen, worried that perhaps I should speak. I didn't. I stood stupidly staring, or following the custom – I wasn't sure.

He asked if I would like some tea. I heard myself answer, "Yes."

We sat down at a small table on his porch. He poured the tea. It was weak and pleasant-tasting. He asked me my name and I said, "Carolyn White."

He looked at me strangely, as if I had given him pause to think. Then he introduced himself as Tomas Byanca. It was strange; my grandfather's name was Thomas as well.

I looked at my host and knew beyond doubt this man was indeed the Hopi spiritual leader.

We drank our tea in silence. At last he remarked that he had noticed me walking past his house. He paused for some time. Then he said he had been watching me watch the sun rise and set each day. He said something about the hill that I can't remember. I said nothing at all. I only spoke if he asked me a question and then I answered as anyone might do while drinking tea with someone new in town. Mostly we sat enjoying the day and sipping tea.

When we were done, he excused me. I thanked him for the tea. Joe had said it was all right to say thank you.

I walked back to the truck in a state of awe. I had hoped for so much and had received so much more. I had met the challenge I had set for myself. Tomas Byanca had recognized me with a tea ceremony; we had drunk from the water's edge. This was for me a formal acknowledgement of my acceptance into the culture of man. It wasn't the words we shared. It was the space between the words, the day, the companionship, the tea, the porch and the ceremony.

It was between the thoughts
between the sky
even between my own intent
and it was enough.

His silences spoke to me and said, "It takes time. If you have a way with the community of horses, you have a way with the community of man. In all people there is a free spirit like a horse. Speak to that spirit and they will listen."

I was truly on my path of Two Worlds Walking.

Thank you to

Verde Valley School

Joe Brown

The Hopi Nation

And Tomas Byanca

Chapter XXV

The Song of the Meadow

The Day I Learned the Language of Wild Horses

Now that I have shared my experiences from the Verde Valley
School study program on the Hopi reservation, you will better
understand my third summer with the wild horses. Joe Brown gave
me the rules that I was expected to follow respecting the cultural
values of the Hopi community. From following these rules, I had to
wait for an invitation and learn patience. I could have gone to Hopi
spiritual leader Tomas Byanca and spoke to him right away. But
what would I have gained, and what would he have said to me? I
am sure there would not have been any tea offered to me. From the
"pause" on the hill I was able to stage my intent, creating the draw
from honoring the laws of the Hopi culture and respect for the
Hopi spiritual leader Tomas Byanca. My waiting was a ceremony of
respect, and the tea ceremony was acknowledgment of my honorable intent. The honor we had for each other opened up the lines of
communication as we sat sipping tea.

If I had not waited and suffered through my own impatience, I
would not have found anything sacred in our meeting. Without
proper respect I would not have been able to gain insight into what
I was looking for. I benefited from my experience in many ways. I
could not have written a large paper on my experience and gotten
the highest mark in school if I had not struggled with the "pause"
on the hill and learned that I could take my own horrendous feelings and turn them to ecstasy. Finding my inner self from having to
be patient has helped me throughout my life.

I learned from the "pause" that I could create a magnetic connection by honoring the natural progress of the relationship to take
place. This is the way it is to speak to the spirit of a horse. You must

wait for him to come to you. Magnetism must be present before communication can begin. This kind of respect is beneficial in all forms of relationships and communication, be they horse or human.

The story I am about to share with you could not have taken place without my understanding of the importance of the "pause" and the natural progress of relationship. The natural progress of time is a ceremony of nature that must be honored for harmonious communication. A spiritual connection can be gained when the natural progress of time is allowed to unfold, respecting and understanding it as a ceremony. This is the formula to an instant rapport. The instant rapport in nature comes from waiting to be invited, after your intentions are understood as honorable. Following this law will bring harmonious communication and friendship upon the first meeting.

I was totally committed to waiting for an invitation from the wild horses to join them. Connecting with nature as I did on that particular day took countless days when nothing happened between the horses and myself. Waiting for the wild horses paralleled my being able to meet with Tomas Byanca the Hopi spiritual leader.

It is befitting to return to the wild horses the day that I experienced the break into their world from a very powerful moment in nature. An accidental, yet perfect timing of "pause" followed, and an accidental act on my part caused the wild horses to accept me into their community.

I was alone in the meadow listening to the wafting air and watching millions of blades of grass turn into a single flowing form. The breeze created shadows, appearing like interchanging colors of flowing ribbons in pastel shades of green and yellow hues.

I couldn't wait until they got there and yet, I reveled in my solitude, perched in the perfection of anticipation and my own personal moment in the meadow. Then, out of nowhere, they arrived, bursting into the field with the energy of laughing children as they found their spot and place within the herd, sharing with each other the meadow and the joy of a perfect day.

The song of the meadow is heard when its shifting breezes race in swirling patterns. The grasses rush across the meadow hand in hand, singing songs that can best be heard in solitude. Golden was my hour spent waiting for their footsteps to appear on the meadow's edge.

The field came alive with their presence. The horses' high spirit from the cool summer wind was causing them to pose and show off, leaping, prancing and bowing their necks and tossing their manes into the air. Their tails looked like fountains in the wind. The meadow looked like an active sea and the horses' dance kept them on the current.

In celebration of their freedom in nature, they were still under constant control. They were controlled by the wind, the moving meadow floor, their need to stay vigilant for predators and their relationship to each other. And in all of that control they were effortless in their celebration of joy.

From the horses' spirit, everything became a dance to my eye – the meadow, the wild horses and my thoughts. I was touched by the coincidence of my reflected thoughts and the herd's artful arrival and how magical they stepped into the rhythm of the flowing grass.

I sat watching nature's ballet and began clapping my hands in delighted appreciation. The sound let the horses know where I was in the meadow. Inadvertently, and purely by accident, my applause had also transported me in an instant into their community.

The horses oddly responded to me like I was one of them. I had finally made it into their world, though I did not understand what possessed them to include me. They began communicating with me like they did with each other. The horses responded to my clapping much the same as a person responds to someone knocking on a door.

At the sound of my clapping, each of the horses moved forward to welcome me into their world. I soon discovered I had made a statement of some kind to the horses. In their eyes I was proclaiming my territorial rights. I used a universal language of all animals that use sound in rhythm, like the thump of a rabbit's foot or the scolding of a squirrel, the croaking of a frog or the stamping hooves of a stallion expressing his territorial rights. The horses in an instant understood I was not a predator. Predators would not call attention to themselves. They would hide and wait for an opportunity to get closer. The horses, like the camel that came to me in the desert, heard my exuberance. They recognized that I was but a playful, innocent youth celebrating my joy of their arrival.

The herd responded and one by one they came to visit me in a greeting ceremony, each in his own way, some with a wandering stride in my direction, others with an arched neck to be closer without commitment. Still others came close while grazing and acknowledged me with a stamped hoof declaring their space right next to mine. All of them shared eye contact with me that said, "I hear you and your declaration, I accept your presence and we will know each other some day in the time of the waiting."

But the most remarkable horse was the one that came up behind me and gently shared my space to see what I was looking at, purposefully touching me with his whiskers and pausing with me far past the time of reason. It was strange; we had never been this close and I did not know where it would lead. I would be careful to stay in waiting so that the time ahead would bring us to a closer connection.

That afternoon, I was becoming aware of many patterns of shared energy between the horses and the meadow. Companionship flowed through the herd and as the meadow breeze turned each blade of grass into a single rippling form, we became family. My ability to see the unity of the movement that surrounded me in nature and how the horses were influenced by their environment brought me to an ability to talk to them in their own language.

I found the formula into the horses' world. It was simple; it was my job to wait for the horses to respond and acknowledge my presence. I had to be in a proper state of bliss, but that is easy for a child. Joyfulness in nature is very appealing to horses and it drew them to me. The horses accepted me into their world when I could see the connection of the grass, the wind and the herd interacting in complete unison. In that moment, I saw their life as herbivores and how natural it was for them to be influenced by their environment. The need to survive and stay on watch could be done not only with fear but also in celebration.

As I stayed in the meadow, I watched and observed the herd for the rest of the day. Horses standing head to tail helped each other keep away the flies. Some horses stood head to head, whiskers touching, a sign of love and affection that I had not understood until that day. It felt the same as when Mustang embraced me in the sway of his neck, holding me there and yet hardly touching me at all. I started noticing couples of horses standing very close, exactly nose to nose, tail to tail, like salt and pepper shakers. Many times, they found a friend who looked identical to their own phenotype and color, and many brothers and sisters united for naps together in the afternoon sun.

Looking across the meadow into the sea of horses now moving

around like a marketplace full of shoppers, I noticed Moonlight standing alone, just days away from foaling. She wasn't grazing. She looked uncomfortable and out of place with the rest of the herd. Everyone avoided her. As I sat in the meadow watching her, wishing I could ease her discomfort and loneliness, Mustano walked up to her and said hello with his concerned breath and quiet charm. He positioned himself by her side and stood with her, sharing her discomfort for the rest of the afternoon. Not once did he ever concern himself with his need to graze. They half closed their eyes, not to open them for the next few hours.

I had recently added a new word to my vocabulary. Anthropomorphism means to attach human qualities to animals and it is usually seen in a negative light. However, I personally had rarely seen the behavior Mustano was exhibiting in my own society, so I felt I wasn't guilty of it in this case. I have since decided that seeing human qualities in animals is a good thing that has truly enriched my life and philosophy.

As I look back on my experience, I realize the meadow, the wilderness and the wild horses gave me the knowledge that everything is connected to everything else in body, mind and spirit. Living in the community of wild horses and being accepted into the herd gradually gave me a greater knowledge of horses than any observation I could have made by looking at the differences between humans and equines. I really only looked for the unity I might share with them. At this point in my experience with their community, I could feel their acceptance of me slowly and surely unfolding as naturally as if I were in a foreign country learning its language and customs. I assimilated their language and culture not through books or word of mouth, but by appreciating what it took for them to survive, honoring their space, waiting for their trust and mimicking their behavior.

The first behavior I copied from the herd was the behavior the horses used most often. This behavior was to alert the herd to suspicious changes in their immediate environment. They were acutely aware of any changes that could be caused by a predator approaching their territory. Each member of the herd had a role to play, namely, to be on guard and warn others of possible danger.

Wild horses are aware that an unfamiliar sound or an unusual quietness often signals danger. Sudden noises or a sudden silence both suggest a possible predator in the area. When I became aware of these warning signs and when I began to use these warning signs to alert the horses, they responded to my concerns as if I were one of them.

When the horses heard a new sound in or around the meadow, they raised their heads to listen. If I heard a sound or sensed any form of trouble, I lifted my head and looked in the direction of my concern, the way I had seen them do. The horses acknowledged me by lifting their heads. If I moved out and away from the sound, they took my lead. To get this response, I had spent many hours responding to their warning signs first. Little by little, they started paying attention to my signals. I don't think it came from me improving my body language. I think it came from a deep connection that was formed over time, one that was created by time and my ever vigilant focus in responding to them.

Their response to me was a hallmark. It was the first time the horses "listened" to my body language and opinions when I meant to communicate a message. It only made sense that this breakthrough should come through my signaling danger since horses are prey animals. I spent the better part of the summer communicating with them every time I heard a noise or a sudden lull in the normal, natural activity of wildlife surrounding the meadow. I tried to get a reaction from each horse. Even though I was at the bottom of the pecking order, my new behavior developed more introductions into the family unit and earned me more respect. I stopped feeling like an island alone, away from civilization. My focus created a heightened awareness of nature that over a period of time became natural for me.

From this connection, the land became a breathing organ and the meadow was the heart and pulse of the communities that shared its ecosystem.

I started realizing that most body movement was conversation. To join the conversation, I learned to use my body movements like humans use facial expressions to communicate without words. The horses spoke to me through their behavior, and their behavior became meaningful to me through the body language we now shared.

I was learning how to speak to horses. I had thought it would come to me from body language in single words like hello, yes or no; I never thought it would come in full sentences in the form of a question.

Suddenly one of the horses in the herd raised its head and looked across the meadow at a stand of trees on the border. From this signal I realized the horse was speaking to me as one person would speak to another. "Did you hear that?" he whispered and I raised my head to look across the meadow to the origin of the sound. In the pause of silence, I answered back. Without intent and before thought, by raising my head, I communicated, "Yes, I did."

Again, another horse spoke from the whiskered touch, pausing with me in the meadow to see what I was looking at. He said to me, "I see you are looking at the two taking a nap. Nice day, isn't it?" We stood in the sound of silent watchfulness, remembering always to listen.

The conversations we shared together were changing the herd's attitude toward me. I was talking to them through an invisible connection, a silent language, in full sentences. I could finally explain the difference between human and equine speech. Horses speak in silence, never forgetting to listen.

From the body language we shared together, yet another communication system developed. Soon we communicated apart from any body language or movement; we communicated in the gap, that silent space between interactions. I believe it was a kind of telepathy that was created from the bond we felt for one another.

The day in the meadow started the process of using the language of horses. The day left me with a feeling of joy. That night, as I lay in bed waiting to fall asleep, I listened to the pine trees rustling up against the cabin and to the distant breezes sailing through the tree tops like the sounds of the seashore. I drifted off to sleep in the arms of the whispering pines, a sound as gentle as the touch of horses' whiskers upon my face. All night I purposely slept lightly to enjoy the sweet songs of the night. I lay waiting for another day in the meadow.

Carolyn Resnick

Chapter XXVI

The Pecking Order Incident

Water Hole Rituals

Years ago, wild water in streams was pure and clean and safe to drink if it ran over the rocks in a streambed for just a short distance. This was true even with the stream the horses used, and I never carried a canteen in the mountains. The water was sweetened from the herbs living along the sandy banks: horsetail, watercress, mint, and a host more whose names I didn't know; but I tasted them and knew them as herbs. Herbs have a special look and they seasoned the water with heavenly flavors. The water also was infused with the essence of loam, creating a taste similar to the flavor of truffles.

I learned the wisdom of the lead horse's language at the place where the horses chose to drink. At the water's edge, pecking order is a language of law and acceptance where rules are desirable and companionship mandatory. The way horses approach the water hole makes their language as clear as the streams they share. Wild horses approach water with great care; for the safety of the herd, they follow pecking order behavior to stay alert to predators.

Mustano, Moonlight, and the other dominant horses chose to drink first. When they finished, they would stand guard and the lower ranking horses would take their turns. There was good reason for the dominant horses to drink first. The less aggressive horses never involve themselves in community service. If they drank first, they would not stand guard afterward.

In all social interactions there is a matrix of pecking order. When we first watch pecking order behavior, we see only its primitive aspect and seemingly unfair justice to the weak. Pecking order seems like a random instinctual behavior that lacks consideration for the weaker animal, almost a callous, mechanical behavior. Only after many years of observing does the underlying purpose and reasons for pecking order become apparent. As the purpose of pecking order becomes more comprehensible, our first evaluation of it changes; in fact, we develop the opposite opinion of it. A horse can be ruthless one moment and as gentle as a caring mother the next. In pecking order interaction, it is easier to see the ruthlessness first.

In using pecking order, horses can display behavior as diverse as gentleness and ruthlessness. How gently Sagebrush could take grass from my hand one moment and in the next instant savagely bite a horse that ventured into our territory. How differently horses can respond in seconds – from tender moments to full aggression. To get a desired response from a horse, like Mustano, I would have to have the body language skills of a mime. I would need the understanding of a leader, the tact of a diplomat, the intuition of a mother, the fairness of an umpire, the eyes of an eagle and the judiciousness of a horse. Mustano had developed these skills and abilities to their highest level and used them to direct a wide range of herd interactions with the skill of a conductor leading a perfectly orchestrated performance.

I was now going to test what I had learned to see if I could get the horses to accept me into the herd. The horses and I were friends, but I was still not a family member, nor would I be until they brought me into their pecking order rituals.

I chose the water hole to make my entrance into the pecking order by declaring my rank and leadership ability. I felt the water hole would be best because the horses were most alert to pecking order interactions there. Anywhere else, they might mistakenly think I was acting as a predator. I knew that at the water hole they would see my aggressive body language display as an attempt to set my rank and earn my rightful position as a family member in their community. I had gained the acceptance and trust of the horses by remaining at the bottom of their pecking order. Up until now, I had no rank. All the horses were fond of me but none of them respected me; even the roans would chase me away if I didn't wait my turn for a drink.

I didn't know if they would accept a human as a herd member. I knew that I would not ask anything they didn't demand from each other, but I felt that not being a horse, my body language might not be understood. My attempts to communicate might elicit a negative response from the whole herd.

If they didn't understand my intent, there could be grave consequences, like the poor horses that came too close to Sagebrush. In the worst case, the rights I did have with the horses would be taken away, but I knew it was worth the risk. The walls were coming down between the horses and myself and the horses were becoming more aggressive toward me everyday. If I waited any longer, it would be too late. The horses would soon become too aggressive to allow me to hold any rank in the pecking order at all. It was now time for me to establish my position in the herd and earn the horses' respect.

It was in the afternoon. The horses walked down the well-worn trail in their usual pattern with the lead horses in front and me trailing a respectable distance behind the roans. We came to the water hole and the horses began drinking. After the last of the horses were drinking, I fell into the movement of a horse, walking with a determined stride. I found a big tree branch to make a statement my small frame wouldn't be able to muster, especially when the horses knew I had little authority to begin with. I snuck up to surprise the roan at the bottom of the pecking order. I swung my branch and splashed water at her. To my astonishment she leaped into the air and took off running. This started a chain reaction; one of the bay mares started chasing her, and Mustano came after me. I high-tailed it up the embankment.

Mustano stopped chasing me almost as soon as he started, so I turned and ran down the embankment again. I ran headlong into Moonlight, and she was not in a good mood. She picked up where Mustano had left off and I took off running again. She was much more persistent than Mustano. I guess she wanted to prove to me that if I was thinking of changing my status in the herd, I would be taking orders from her.

Moonlight chased me around the bushes and rocks with her neck stretched out, pointing her nose at me, stamping her feet and rolling her eyes. I was running out of breath and wondering if my time on earth was over. After all, everything I was doing was experimental and I had no idea of how it would turn out.

When she stopped chasing me and headed back to the herd, I followed her. Every so often she turned her head to look at me. I responded to her the way I had seen other horses do by stopping and waiting for permission to follow her. I hoped that Mustano would not take exception to my return, because I had no breath left. Moonlight had run me ragged.

When we rejoined the herd, Mustano greeted us with an arched neck and proudly walked up to me. I extended a hand to him. He reached out his nose and smelled my hand for a few moments. When he stopped smelling my hand, I walked over and joined the horses in the field. With Mustano's approval, I had permission to join the herd. This time, I was truly a part of the herd, second from the bottom in pecking order.

I was elated. Watching how the herd moved around and related to each other in common bonding and pecking order behavior had paid off. I had graduated into the family of horses.

The mare that I had contested at the waterhole I named Little River. She was more than happy to let me go ahead of her at the waterhole thereafter. During the next few months, I worked my way up the pecking order ladder in the same fashion I had at the water hole. I also established grazing rights by laying claim to certain areas of the fields, like Sagebrush had done with her thorn bushes. The tactics I used were the rules the horses used. First, I could not challenge another horse if he or she was alert to my whereabouts. Secondly, when I made my challenge it had to be a surprise attack.

I continued to set myself to the task of challenging the horse ahead of me in the pecking order, looking to increase my rank. Most of the time, when the horse I challenged ran, another mare would take off after her, supporting me in my bid.

After I established leadership with Sagebrush, I had only Moonlight and Mustano to challenge pecking order rites. When I started my quest for a position in the herd, I did not know where I would end up. I soon discovered that my success did not come from winning battles, as much as taking advantage of the higher-ranking horse's lack of focus. This was a phenomenal discovery that went against everything I had ever heard about pecking order.

It was also the reason I couldn't challenge Moonlight. Moonlight knew where I was at all times, making it impossible to surprise her. This is the way it is with lead horses; it is why lead horses stay leaders. It comes from their acute focus on everything around them. Moonlight gave me no reason to contest her at the water hole and no chance, either. Since she always knew where I was, I could never sneak up on her.

To my surprise, when I surpassed Sagebrush in the pecking order, Moonlight took a liking to me. She came to my defense in many disputes I had with other horses. She came up to me a lot to say hello. Moonlight, Sagebrush and I became best of friends.

In a short time, the horses were treating me like I was a horse. If I did not keep a sharp eye, a horse might threaten me with a bite or a kick. I found my place in the pecking order was third from the top. As I developed my ability to gain rank with the herd, I discovered my communication skills grew as well. I was now able to talk to the horses with body signals and send and receive telepathic messages that replaced their need of a spoken language.

I could now lead the herd within reason. To do this, I needed Mustano and Moonlight's interest in following me. If they thought it was a good idea, they would signal the herd and the herd would then follow my lead.

At the water hole I discovered how to come up through the ranks. By the time I was third in command, I had learned that the more order there is in a herd, the greater the herd's ability to communicate.

Before rank has been agreed upon and a leader has been chosen, the herd's communication system is lacking; the horses have access to only a rudimentary vocabulary and a few basic phrases. In establishing the pecking order, the horses create their real language. The movements they invent in sorting out their rights develops a language rich enough to communicate ideas, thoughts, wishes, romance and concepts that have nothing to do with pecking order whatsoever.

Humans have a hard time communicating with horses because they haven't gone through these rituals to develop a language they can share with a horse. Until a person participates in these pecking order rituals and achieves some status within the herd, the horses will never understand him as well as they understand other horses.

I deciphered the horses' pecking order code at the water hole. I went alone and told no one where I was going. At the water hole, I found the key to the language and trust of horses. Once I could communicate with the horses through formal pecking order games, the horses picked up my language as quickly as I picked up theirs.

Looking back I realized I had learned the language of horses and had became as versed in that language as Mustano. Horse communication is not like our own language. English requires no personal qualities of character to be understood, but for horses to respond to me and understand what I was saying, I had to get in touch with my own virtues, horse instincts and horse sense. The horses led me to discover the instinctive reasoning of animals, which is their natural ability to problem-solve that comes from instinct and conscious choice working together. The herd knew when community rights should supersede individual rights and when individual rights should supersede community rights. They raised me like a young foal, guiding me into the ways of horses and into a community consciousness that was made up from the best each individual had to offer.

I had to demonstrate my interest in companionship and need for community, and if I didn't, the horses would chastise me with judicious desertion. Wild horses taught me that everything in life is a partnership. When there is no loss of community in the act of communication, rapport is the result. The circle of communication must be present both in speaking and listening before there can be any understanding with horses.

The process of learning horse language revealed the desire horses have to follow a leader without question. It made it possible to lead them without force or capture. In finding this true language of horses, I discovered the meaning of charisma and how to win a horse's trust. The horses became deeply devoted and took my direction in the instant I requested it.

At the end of the last day of my second summer, my thirst led me down to the creek. I found a perfect spot. As I was bending over the water, I heard a horse approaching. In the water's reflection, I saw Mustano standing behind me. He felt I was leaving and had come to say goodbye. He used the water's reflection to gaze into my eyes. I moved over to give him room. He stepped to the creek's edge and dipped his nose in the fresh, uncrossed, wild water. We were now family. He approved of me and told me so by sharing a drink with me. Until that day, he would not have allowed this act.

I have never forgotten the drink we shared at the water's edge with eyes glued on each other, because we both knew it tasted better that way.

Chapter XXVII

Boulder Ritual
Symbiosis

The morning held a promise of warmth to come, but at 8 AM I was cold in the meadow. So I moved up into some boulders that bordered the meadow. These boulders were like comfortable living room furniture. They trapped the warmth of the sun, providing many different sizes and shapes of cozy chairs and hammocks. The contrast between the chilly morning and reflected warmth off the boulders removed my desire to do anything but relax.

Standing on one of the boulders, looking for the right place to sit, I noticed Moonlight coming up the hill. She couldn't resist the warm atmosphere of the boulders, and besides, she wanted to see what I was doing. I was careful not to make any sudden movements that might change her attitude or direction. I kept very still as she began smelling my feet that were just above her eye level. I slowly lowered myself until I was sitting on one of the boulders. I was still above her head, so I lowered myself the rest of the way to the ground, being careful not to frighten her away.

I was standing right next to her when she backed up against one of the boulders and started rubbing her tail. I took the opportunity to scratch her tail to help her out. She had developed many places on her body that itched from summer bug bites. Little by little, I was able to scratch her all over her body. She felt strong and she was white as snow. This was the first time she allowed me to touch her. Just like that – I could not believe my good fortune. Little did I know it would lead to trouble.

She turned her body to the places she wanted to have groomed. Then she backed into me so she could increase the pressure – and that is when the trouble began. Wedging me between two boulders,

223

she backed up and pushed me into the rocks, stepping on my toes in the process. In an instant, my pleasant surroundings became an inescapable vice. I was trapped but afraid to object for fear she might kick. She kept stepping on me, rubbing back and forth, back and forth, until she was satisfied.

When she had finished grooming, my toes were swollen. I did not know how I would get my boots off. They felt two sizes too small. I was worn out and concerned. The horses were all starting to itch from the heat and fly bites. I realized they might come to expect me to groom them as well. I pictured all the horses chasing me down to get their daily scratch. Moonlight and I were going to have to work out some details. It was time to set some social rules for our relationship.

I started the next day meeting Moonlight out in the open so she could not pin me against anything. When she came to me she was all ready to have me groom her again. But this time she was not going to be able to abuse me like she had. While scratching her tail, if she backed up to increase the pressure, I could walk backwards. When she forced me to back up to avoid her stepping on my feet, I stopped grooming her. She then quickly learned to stand still or I would quit grooming. In a short time I had turned the tables and I was now in charge. I was then able to communicate to her other things I needed her to do for her grooming like moving to the left or right or moving forward and turning around. Through her interest in grooming, I soon had her performing integrated movements.

What I was learning is that magic and instant rapport don't come overnight. The horses were less afraid of me, but that created new problems.

This problem was really a blessing. It was actually the first step many horsemen use in breaking and training a horse before riding it, except that in this case the horse experienced the interaction as enjoyable. The method I am referring to is called "sacking a horse out." A horse trainer will tie up a horse, then violate the horse's body by rubbing or beating a sack against the horse's coat until the horse becomes desensitized to the process and realizes there is no pain connected to it. Many people call this "gentling a horse." But the way I figure it, I have no right to make a horse experience something against his will when he has no recourse, especially if there is another way to accomplish the same goal. I want our relationship to be mutually developed without ropes or ties or fences or any restraint. In the beginning, all these gentling techniques cause extreme fear in the horse. I want our relationship to grow naturally, without fear.

Moonlight needed to figure out that she had to change her behavior if she was to get any more grooming from me. I brought about this change by agreeing to grooming only when she was in an open field. That way she couldn't trap me to her cause. If she became aggressive and tried to push me down, I stopped grooming her. When she relaxed, I would resume grooming. If she didn't listen, I'd walk or run away. She had to figure out how to work as a team, and from this, we developed a common language.

What I did with Moonlight takes a little longer than sacking a horse out – a few days, perhaps – but during that time, I developed a common language with Moonlight that allowed us to work together. Sacking a horse out might gentle it, but it adds little training. My method of dealing with Moonlight develops teamwork and a horse's ability to take direction from me on many levels. In only a few days, I taught Moonlight to step forward, step back, step left, step right, and halt, all on my command. She was more than willing to follow my direction while I was grooming and gentling. These teamwork requests would serve me well when it was time to ride her.

Developing teamwork with Moonlight caused me to wonder about the symbiotic relationships between species and how they develop. How did the hippo come to hold his mouth open to allow little birds to pick his teeth clean? How did the honey-bird and honey badger arrive at their mutually beneficial relationship? Even before my experience with the wild horses, I saw these symbiotic relationships as proof that the same type of relationship is possible with a horse. I could see that these symbiotic connections come from a natural process through the mutual needs of two unlike creatures – as happened between Moonlight and me. I believed she would not object to me mounting and riding her if she had it in her mind that riding her was a part of the grooming experience.

The day in the boulders with Moonlight gave me the chance to learn how to relate to a horse in a natural way. In those days we spent together, we became very close. We both got to know each other well. From those days, I developed my skill that helped me throughout my life as a trainer, breeder and communicator. What took place next was what I was hoping to gain, the ability to ride a wild horse from a natural bond.

Chapter XXVIII

Invitation to Ride

Companion Energy

My dad said, "If there is unity in the moment with the horse, you can direct his next movement with aids almost as light as a thought, like geese flying in formation. Do geese practice how to be united? No! They just are. It comes naturally from the bond they share together." He went on to say that harmonious acts seldom lead to trouble.

Moonlight and I had developed a bond. We understood our boundaries and trusted each other. But no matter how close we had become, she was still a wild horse in total control of everything we did together.

On the day I rode Moonlight, she maintained a higher rank than my own and I knew it would always be that way. But I took a chance and put my faith in my father's formula. And he was right.

The horses were grazing in the field and I was playing in the boulders when I saw Moonlight coming up the hill to greet me. I walked down to say hello, then we headed back to the boulders together. I climbed up on a boulder. She came up to the boulder and turned her body sideways as if to a mounting block. She stood still, exposing an opportunity that no horse-loving girl could refuse. Wild or not, I was getting on. I eased onto her back.

There I was on top of Moonlight for the first time. She felt like an ocean wave to me. A wave cannot be controlled but it can be ridden. That is just how Moonlight felt. I was catching a ride on Moonlight with no ability to control her, like a surfer's inability to change the course of the wave. The bond was set.

She waited for a moment, bent her neck around and smelled my feet, raised her head and took a good look at me sitting on her. She paused another moment, then started walking back to the herd.

I was a passive passenger on a wild mustang's back going on an adventure few people have ever experienced. My belief was true, my belief that horses are born with a desire to be ridden. This day was proving to me that it was possible to ride on the back of a wild horse without the need of training, from an invitation rather than from capture.

I sat on her back noticing the subtle differences in her movement as she walked and how her barrel felt between my legs. No other ride had ever felt this way to me. She felt different because it was her idea for me to ride on her back. I could feel her working with me to keep me in harmony with her stride. It was similar to the time Ora had let me ride on his retired reining horse at his ranch, similar to the first time I rode a carousel horse, even similar to riding my own horse, Mustang. This experience was similar to every great moment I'd ever had on a horse's back. Riding Moonlight was the culmination of all the best riding I'd ever done in my life, and more.

I felt both a connection with her and an unfamiliarity that didn't fit with my vision of what this experience would be like. It was better than my dream.

As she walked toward the field that separated the herd from the boulders, I realized I had accomplished my goal in the time frame I had given myself, though I had no idea how it was going to work out. Her invitation convinced me that horses do have a desire to be ridden without domination, capture or restraint. If those methods were the only means to riding horses, I would have given up riding.

Horses relate to me and reveal a personality that they show no one else. I have read books on understanding the character of horses by the shape of the ears and eyes and skull, the dish in the head, and the size of the nose. These qualities of confirmation play no part in my relationship with a horse. I know the horse as an individual. I have learned to speak to a horse's spirit. I have discovered that inside every horse are hundreds of personalities. I bring out the personality that likes me best.

As Moonlight and I entered the field, I reached down and scratched her neck, shoulders and withers and said, "Whoa." She stopped. I clucked and she started walking again. I tried this several times and each time she responded in the same manner. I was surprised and pleased with her reaction to my requests. She had learned these signals from our grooming sessions.

Even though I could stop her and ask her to move on, I soon discovered I had no control of where we were going. It was obvious we were heading right at the herd and I panicked. Moonlight wanted to show me off to her friends.

When the herd first sighted us, they stood as still as statues in the park. Then they pranced around and stopped to take another look in disbelief. I felt it was important to play the scene out with her. I had to show her my complete faith and trust. So I sat tight. Then several horses took off running. A few came trotting up to us. These were the ones that most concerned me. I thought a squabble might ensue because of the disruption we were causing and we might accidentally be kicked. I hoped the fact that Moonlight was the lead mare would help control the restless crowd surrounding us.

Mustano showed no concern, which encouraged the other horses to return. There was so much excitement around us, I had little time to consider my predicament. After several harrowing moments, the herd became more curious than alarmed. Once they recognized it was Moonlight and I and not some strange creature with two heads, they realized that Moonlight was not disturbed by having me on her back. Soon they became amused and settled down to enjoy the spectacle.

I felt joy, fear, accomplishment and surprise, but I guess the feeling that stood out most was my connection and love for all these wonderful beings that had accepted me as part of their family. I felt like leaning over and hugging Moonlight then leaping off her back and hugging the whole herd. But instead, I just sat still and savored my first invitation to ride on the back of a wild mustang, wanting to remember these moments for the rest of my life.

Then, as nonchalantly as we had arrived, Moonlight turned and headed back to the boulders, still taking great care to balance my body in unison with her stride. The herd followed us from a distance in a single line. Moonlight took me back to the boulder where I had mounted her. I slid off her back. As I stood on the boulder, all the horses gathered around us. They smelled me and smelled Moonlight's back. Moonlight wandered off to graze and I sat down in the crowd of horses as they inspected me with their whisker-touching and gentle breath.

The herd milled pleasantly around me like a weekend museum crowd, all being respectful and patiently waiting their turn to have a closer look at me. They wanted to inspect me from the new point of view acquired by seeing me on Moonlight.

My last summer unfolded my dreams of riding wild horses. Each horse chose a time to be alone with me. With some I went on meditation walks. Others asked for grooming, as Moonlight had done. During these individual interactions, several horses asked me upon his or her back.

Finding the secret to riding a wild horse from a bonded trust came from my understanding of harmony. Harmony is not made, it is found. Harmony in nature is the most trusted element in life and is the basis of the success I share with horses.

Everyone has experienced moments when everything feels right or safe, a moment that makes you feel you will live forever. These moments I have no name for, but they can be trusted. They are all around us every minute. The trick is to recognize these moments and act upon them. In these moments, it is possible to ride on the back of a wild horse just like I did.

I have never shared this story before. It was too precious. I feared the telling would diminish the magic of the experience or even lose the memory, but I now feel it is important and needs to be told.

Words are hard to find, especially when words played no part in the happening. I am sharing my story now in hopes it will spark new ideas and bring more understanding and love for horses and for all animals. When I look to the future of wild horses today, I am deeply concerned. I feel we are missing the importance of our relationship to horses and our need for them. Through the conscious act of remembering and honoring them, we not only protect the horses, we protect human society and its goodness.

Humans have debts to nature and to everything that lives on the earth. If we do not honor these debts, we will not honor our own community. We may in fact conquer the world but destroy ourselves in the process.

From the wisdom and kinship of wild horses I became a student in the ways of nature and developed a deep awareness and need for companionship and community well being.

When the community is at peace, so is the individual. I learned a greater understanding of my own language that is deeper by far than the dictionary definition of a word.

I miss Mustang, Mustano, Moonlight, and the whole herd at

Hurky Creek. As long as there are wild horses racing on open lands, I feel their presence. I see them in fields, on pathways, in creeks and streams and in the eyes of every horse I meet. When I look back, their names begin to flow like rivers.

Miwok, Hopi, Sara, Sunshine, River Walk, Amber Lace, Sweetie Pie, Buckeye, Choctaw, Cochise, Sagebrush, Blue Lake, Red Wing, Little Fire, Silhouette, Devil's Claw, Painted Lady, Ruby, Sunny Boy, Rosebud, Hurky, Socks, Moonlight, Mustano, Bell, Long Shadow, Kick, Romeo, Paloma, Sultan, El Capitan, Diamante, Gavilan, Chico, Chewie, Mariposa, Kachina, Zuni, Comanche, Serena, Windy, Cody, Banshee, Wind Song, L.B., Dusty, Brewster, Running Deer, Little River, Blackstone, Bright Star, Romance, My Little Girl, Remember Me, Sally, Dolly, Blue Diamonds, Dancer, Blue Eyes, Rebel, Whiskers. They are gone now, but forever remembered in my heart.

The wild horses gave me a deep need to create more interest in humans to discover that there are natural laws that can support the individual to a greater strength. Through my life's work with horses I am bringing attention to the fact that pecking order has qualities of merit in achieving a unified herd in a harmony that supports the weakest individual from a wild horse's sense of duty to the herd. They have a phenomenal ability to work together as a team through balancing their needs between community rights and individual rights, something that does not come easily to humankind. It is my life's work to bring a clear understanding of the social order of wild horses in nature to humanity. We could greatly improve our communication system, and our quality of support to others as leaders by what we could learn from wild horses.

Epilogue

As I have looked for theories, methods and formulas for the higher forms of horsemanship, my larger interest has always been the connection horses have to each other and the environment. From these interests my horsemanship skills were enhanced to create enchanting performances with horses. I found that the performance which comes from a connection we share together is magical, when aids are thoughts and touches, as light as a fly. My focus for shaping the horse for competition is to develop his interest to have a desire to perform in unity with my direction.

My life with horses has been spent between two worlds: one training for many riding disciplines (from show horses to dressage) and the other studying wild horse behavior. Both worlds have helped me learn about the true nature of horses. Interacting with wild horses led me to an understanding and bond with a horse that is magical. Training horses has created my ongoing studies of leadership and communication, both with horses and in business communicating with people.

There are two worlds: the spiritual and the functional. Those who understand both worlds are on the cutting edge of leadership. Understanding both the spiritual and functional brings an ability to create a meeting ground to establish leadership through teamwork.

Naked Liberty's focus is on how I developed my ability with horses, my understanding of herd society and how dominant horses can be led from their natural instinct to follow a leader without changing their rank to do so. The book reveals my relationship with wild horses through inter species communication. It draws attention to a universal connection through unity with horses and an instant language that is available to all creatures in nature. From interacting and communicating with wild horses in herd groups, I found a code of behavior that we have in common. I learned of a universal language that exists among horses, that extends to all creatures great and small, even to our own family and friends.

My goal is to bring my findings to a common knowledge in order to raise standards of behavior toward animals and standards of behavior toward each other. I want to create public awareness of how horses and all animals enrich our lives and how our relationship with horses and all animals can offer more information that will further benefit humanity. I think that in this modern age we have lost sight of the value and integrity animals have. We do not appreciate animals for what they have to teach us. We have forgotten how much they have impacted our lives. Just as my grandmother said to me as a child, I continue to wonder if we would have invented the airplane had we not seen birds fly, or invented camouflage clothing had we not seen chameleons and other creatures virtually hidden by the patterns of their hide. If it were not for nature and creatures in nature that do things that we cannot, would we have created boats, submarines, cars, tall buildings, music, fire or electricity? We have animals to thank for expanding our horizons of what is possible and what we can achieve.

Unfortunately, our inaccurate perception of animals and our negative opinion of animal behavior have undermined the further benefits we can glean from animals. The insights I have gained from wild horses could change people's perceptions and create a new focus on the lessons that can be learned to improve our growth in community, networking and leadership.

My concern is that negative opinions of animals, or no opinions of them at all, affects the way we deal with them. Not understanding animal behavior, with all its meaning, reason and virtue, causes our cruel behavior toward animals.

If we do not perceive and understand animals correctly, we easily become fearful and defensive. This fear and defensiveness toward nature and animals sets up a subconscious distrust that can play out in our interactions with each other.

An animal can display vicious behavior, but it is my belief that if I deal with that animal in a way that appeals to the better side of his behavior, he will respond to me in a positive way. This attitude has given me the ability to communicate successfully with most all animals.

The reason it is so easy for humans to see nature as predominately violent is that occasional violence in nature brings about drama, action and possible death. However, harmony is the natural condition in nature that often goes unnoticed because it is a calm, quiet, peaceful state of existence. There is no turmoil or chaos in harmony; therefore, we give it little attention. Harmony has not been investigated with as much interest as the ruthless side of nature. I believe that this lack of focus on harmony in nature causes humans to lose interest in the pursuit of harmony and morality in general.

It is my hope that the study of inter species communication will shed more light on the language of horses and all creatures. I would like science to accept inter species communication and learn to use animal language in researching animal behavior. Animals are trying to communicate with us all the time. I would like to see science focus its studies on these communications that are being unnoticed and overlooked. I would like my work with horses to be accepted as Jane Goodall's work with chimpanzees has been.

At the moment, I am completing a how-to book on a formula that will develop skills in creative problem solving, communication and leadership through interacting with horses. The formula is based on the water hole rituals I used as a child to gain the bond that I shared with wild horses.

Today I give private and semiprivate three-day courses to people who are interested in learning the horses' language and social behavior to further their relationships with horses and humans. I also am training selected people who posses natural talent with horses to give clinics on my methods of horse communication and leadership. I am looking forward to doing lectures on the spiritual connection with nature and horses and the functional application of creative leadership and communication.

Beyond my every day life with horses, I still communicate with horses in the wild using horse behavior and the magnetic attraction that horses and humans have in common. I have continued my ongoing relationship with wild horses, advancing my understanding of their society, language and laws of behavior. While I would like my ranch to be large enough to be able to walk with a band of horses that are free on an open range, it is not. However, there is a place I can go where wild horses still run free in family groups; it is called Return to Freedom Wild Horse Sanctuary in Lompoc, California.

The Return to Freedom Sanctuary consists of three hundred acres of rolling paradise devoted to family groups of wild horses. Neda De Mayo, of Return to Freedom, was able to rescue intact families of wild horses. This is most important to my study because wild horses that are put together by people are not a natural wild herd.

Horses that are put together by humans behave differently than if they had the ability to choose their own herd. Throwing horses together creates too many "cooks in the kitchen" in the pecking order. The horses do not produce the genetic offspring they would if they were in the wild and allowed to make their own selections. All of these factors are very important to the studies of wild horses and how they communicate with one other.

Unnatural herd selection can create aggressive pecking order behavior in their communication system. Forced relationships create dysfunctional behavior. The longer a herd has been together, the more sophisticated their communication system becomes. The more sophisticated the system, the more there is to study and the more we can learn from them. Longtime natural bands of horses are magical in their connection.

For several years, Neda De Mayo worked by my side learning my methods, and has continued working with me over the last five years. She is using the knowledge I have shared with her to empower her own original programs. Neda lives the language and laws of horses every day. She inspires me to stay in touch with my dream and is helping my work with horses to find a place in history through her own caring spirit and knowledge.

Beyond the study programs and care for wild horses offered at Return to Freedom, she has become a strong voice for wild horses in America. Neda feels that the American wild horse of today is a vital part of America's cultural heritage and an integral part of the wild habitats they have survived on.

There is a negative public awareness about wild horses. Misinformation and rumor has it that these horses are destroying public lands. Many people forget that the ancestors of the wild horses of today have served people for centuries. Let's remember that we are a nation of people that has been supported throughout our history by the sweat and service of horses. Let's honor their contributions to our lives and the gifted they have contributed to us throughout history. They have carried us, our burdens and helped man create civilizations for centuries. They are entitled to a place to exist on this earth that we all share.

We must take responsibility for the negative conditions wild horses are experiencing if we expect to have a bright future in generations to come. Humane behavior towards all species is the only answer to man's future well being.

It disturbs me to see wild horses taken off range land and separated from their families. The suffering these horses experience is great and never heals. America has enough open land today for the wild horses to live out their lives. We have destroyed the buffalo herds of the past; must the wild horse herds be next?

We could greatly increase our influence, if we who are concerned with the plight of wild horses join together as a united group. The honorable and right thing to do is offer them a compassionate and just existence. We have common laws for wild horses, which due to amendment and policy changes have resulted in the problems wild horses face today. We owe them something more.

In 1971, The Wild Free Roaming Horse and Burro Act passed unanimously with no dissenting votes. It was fueled by great emotional public outcry. Since the act was passed for their protection on our public lands, the wild horses have lost six states where they had designated herd areas for their preservation and hundreds of herds have been zeroed out completely. Once again, America's wild horses need our voice.

"The wild horses that exist today are a re-introduced, native wild life species that have evolved back into a natural state over the last few hundred years on this continent. The birthright of all creatures is freedom. There is nothing more important than preserving our natural resources, our wildlife species and natural habitat. The presence of the American wild horse protects the spirit of the land they roam on." Neda De Mayo.

To learn more about the subject of wild horses and Return To Freedom Wild Horse Sanctuary, visit www.returntofreedom.org, or write:

Return to Freedom
P.O. Box 926
Lompoc, CA 93438

Epilogue

Photo Album

1) The ranch I grew up on as it looked a few years ago.
2) Mustang, my all time favorite horse.

1) I am 14 at the Del Mar show on Chub's Melody, Gladys Foster's Poncho Bueno daughter. I campaigned her heavily for two years undefeated in Western pleasure and trail divisions. Gladys and Chubs were very influential in shaping my success as a competitor. I learned from Gladys that showing is a way of life, not a competition.

2) Strawberry and I with Helen in the Indio Date Festival Parade. I was 7 in this picture. Helen and her husband Buck were good friends to our family and were the caretakers of the Odlum Ranch, which sat next to our ranch.

3) I am 8 years old with my father's horse Flash and Mustang. This is the photo I spoke of at the beginning of Chapter 16. The reason for my grin is that I was hiding a space between my teeth.. I had no idea how to adjust the bridles and bits at this age however the horses were fine with it.

4) I was 14 years of age on my Arabian mare Lover when this picture was taken at the Kelly ranch that sat about a half mile from our ranch. Lover was the first horse I trained from start to a finished bridle horse. In this picture she was a green 4-year-old. By that time I had learned how to adjust my tack.

5) A picture of Flashlight at the gate my dad built. It's the same gate that Mustang used to lock Bryan the Belgian workhorse, away from his mare Babe. This behavior showed me that horses have premeditated behavior, which shows their intelligence.

1) A picture of me at two and a half years old with my grandparents Elsie and Les Martin taken in front of our home in Indio.

2) My Dad and I and my mother's dog Iblese at a Santa Barbara show ground. The horse trailer in the background is one that my dad built.

3) A picture of my mother taken in the 90's.

My Dad with the sherriff posse in the Indio Date Festival Parade.

My Dad and Mustang. This was Mustang's first day being hooked to a cart.

Sweetie Pie and I at the Indio Date Festival Show. At the age of 12 I trained her for the 3 gaited class. Chuck Travis, my coach, taught me how to train a 3 gaited horse from the ground. He never sat on her.

The convoy at Verde Valley School in Sedona, Arizona moments before we left for our trip to the Hopi Reservation.

1) When searching for wild horses in nature I would look for places horses are known to inhabit. Before I would come across the horses I would find traces of their existence, like this grooming branch.

2) Wild horses in a unity of flight exhibiting the magnetic connection in movements that I learned how to use for a harmonious ride.

3) Wild horses in nature exhibiting a one-mind connection that creates the magnetic connection they share together.

The wind was up and I felt totally in unity with the moment and with a herd of wild horses. From these moments in unity I learn the most about how to train horses.

A picture of my student India Gomez riding freely without tack on my Arabian/Quarter Horse cross Navaar, at my ranch in Sonoma. They are exhibiting companion energy and the joy of unity in moments they share together. They are "the picture" of what I have been able to give others from my experiences in the wild and my studies of wild horse behavior.

The area where horses come to drink is a perfect place to study horse behavior in the wild. As a child it is where I learned the social laws horses follow and how pecking order creates a strong working society. These photos I took at the Wild Horse Sanctuary in Shingle Town, California and Mustafa Sabankaya's Ranch in Santa Cruz, California.

A young foal looking for his mother. He is not old enough yet to use the dominant position from behind to influence the horses to make way for him in his search for his mother. His ears are up and he is cautiously weaving his way through the herd.

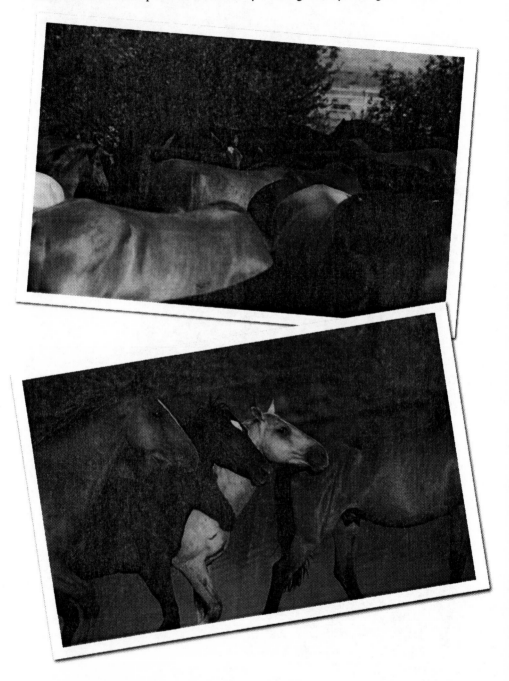

Photo taken seconds before the horse in front was influenced by the three horses behind to move into the trot. This is an example of intentional teamwork using the "dominant push" from behind. The unity in the horses' footsteps and the push from behind is the signal to the horse in front to join them.

An example of how a small confined area can increase terrritorial fighting between horses. These two stallions had been bickering with each other all morning but really got into it when they found they could trap each other in the corner of a fence section.

A wild stallion demonstrating body language of the dominant push from behind; ears back, wrinkled nose, marching steps and lowered head. In this position every horse is willing to follow his directions. He means business and he is not in a good mood. To increase his aggression through body language he would lower his head even further to the ground.

Stony, my exhibition horse, and I at Ray
Hackworth's on our vacation. Photo
taken in the late 70's.

An example of companion walking, one of the seven waterhole rituals.
Stony and I on a morning walk in the mid 80's. We have been together
more than 25 years.

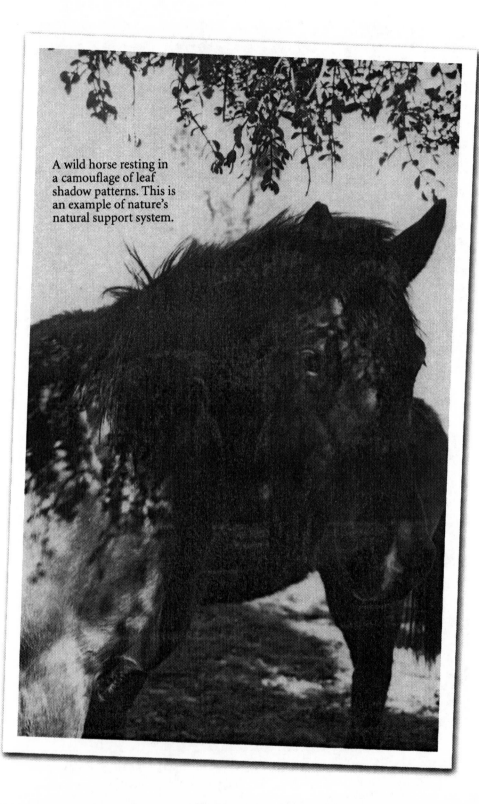

A wild horse resting in a camouflage of leaf shadow patterns. This is an example of nature's natural support system.

Carolyn Resnick

About the Author

Nationally known for her original training methods, her understanding of natural herd behavior, and the remarkable connection that she shares with all horses, Carolyn Resnick's career and studies have spanned over 40 years as a trainer, Arabian breeder, clinician and student of wild horse behavior.

Her life with horses began in Indio, California in the 1940s. Riding alone in the desert as a child, she nurtured an intuitive bond with horses. As a junior rider her interest led to training and showing in both English and Western divisions. Her desire to create a championship performance from the willing spirit of the horse led her on a unique quest to gain knowledge of natural wild horse behavior and communication systems. In the beginning of what would become a lifelong passion for developing innovative horse training methods created from her interactive studies with wild horses, Carolyn spent three summers of her childhood gradually becoming accepted into a community of wild horses.

Carolyn's formal introduction to the wider equine community began in the early 1970s from her ranch, Stonehenge Arabians/Dances With Horses, a successful training and Arabian breeding center in Sonoma, California. She toured the United States for several years, giving clinics and exhibitions on her horse communication system. In addition, Carolyn's Liberty Training video, released in 1988, has impacted the horse community in better relationships with horses.

After 25 years, Carolyn retired from the breeding and training business and moved to a smaller ranch in Escondido, California. Today she coaches dressage and gives private instruction in Liberty Training, Beyond the Whisper™. Her life today also includes serving on the advisory board of Return To Freedom American Wild Horse Sanctuary in Lompoc, California as an expert in wild horse behavior. She is also in the process of developing programs for the business world to enhance leadership communication.

Carolyn Resnick

For additional copies and video contact
Carolyn Resnick / Dances with Horses
1835A S. Centre City Parkway #248
Escondido, CA 92025-6504
www.beyondthewhisper.com
760/743.3377

Carolyn Resnick